Improving
Struggling
Schools

Improving Struggling Schools

A Developmental
Approach
to Intervention

D. BRENT STEPHENS

HARVARD EDUCATION PRESS
CAMBRIDGE, MASSACHUSETTS

Library of Congress Control Number 2009942752

Paperback ISBN 978-1-934742-57-0
Library Edition ISBN 978-1-934742-58-7

Published by Harvard Education Press,
an imprint of the Harvard Education Publishing Group

Harvard Education Press
8 Story Street
Cambridge, MA 02138

Cover Design: Billy Boardman

The typefaces used in this book are Sabon and Formata.

Contents

Acknowledgments   vii

Foreword   *by Michael Fullan*   ix

Introduction   The Instructional Improvement Crisis   1

Part 1   **Struggling Schools: Three Case Studies**

Chapter 1   Stoddard School: Five Years in Intervention   21

Chapter 2   Tanner School: One Year in Intervention   51

Chapter 3   Connington School: Seven Years in Intervention   83

Part 2   **Understanding Intervention's Problems and Potential**

Chapter 4   What's Going Wrong with Intervention?   117

Chapter 5   Creating a Developmental Profile to Assess Schools' Needs   143

Chapter 6   Twelve Steps Toward Supporting Struggling Schools   171

Conclusion   A Developmental Approach to Intervention   197

Notes   209

About the Author   215

Index   217

Acknowledgments

To all of the people who have had a hand in shaping this book, I am deeply grateful. In the course of this writing, over seven years and in many schools, I've had the privilege of hearing the stories of dozens of teachers, principals, and central office administrators—all of whom are working in earnest and with varying degrees of success. Sometimes hopeful, sometimes sad, and occasionally self-defeating, these stories were the starting point for whatever ground I was able to cover in these pages. Education will always be an endeavor centered on people—on children and teachers, mostly—and because of this, its improvement will always resist the fools. The challenge is one of learning, and this is mostly what the rulemakers need to keep in mind.

I owe a special debt to Richard Elmore, who, in a meeting about an early version of this text in which I described the challenges I encountered in the schools I chronicled, asked the simple question that no writer wants to hear: "So what?" It was this challenge to think more deeply about what is going on in low-performing schools, to shift from documenting to problem-solving, that lead to the second half of this book. I'm fortunate that this was only one of many provocative, shaping interactions with him over the last decade.

I also greatly appreciate the guidance of Richard Murnane and Tom Hehir at the Harvard Graduate School of Education. Each offered thoughtful suggestions about this project through all of its phases.

In the Urban Superintendents Program at Harvard, I wish to thank Bob Peterkin and Linda Wing. Bob has served as director of this program for twenty years, and has greatly influenced many educational leaders. The stamp of this program, and the wisdom of both, is something I hope appears in these pages. Among the many members and affiliates of the Urban Superintendents Program, I am especially grateful for the friendship and guidance of Susan Enfield, Brian Osborne, and Holly Weeks; and the generosity of Tom Payzant.

There's no adequate description of the contribution made to me by Karla Baehr. In work, writing, and life, she has been a constant source of inspiration and my model of how to lead with integrity. My deepest thanks to her and to Ann Case for their example and their friendship.

Over the last two years, I've been guided and helped by many wonderful and smart people at Harvard Education Press, including Caroline Chauncey, Marcy Barnes, and Jeff Perkins. This is really a crack unit.

Finally, and certainly most important to me, is the love, patience, and support I've received over so many years from my wife Emily Kolker, daughter Marin, and mother and father. They are the bedrock, and everything else is possible only because of them.

Foreword

Improving Struggling Schools offers a revealing analysis of the failure of school turnaround efforts in the current policy climate. Stephens—a recent graduate of the Urban Superintendents Program at the Harvard Graduate School of Education and an experienced school leader—brings to bear his years of work in urban schools to provide three brilliantly and painfully portrayed case studies that take us deep inside the nitty-gritty of school-based change processes. He draws on these exquisitely detailed portraits to present a compelling vision for the role of external intervention in supporting school improvement.

The stories of the Stoddard, Tanner, and Connington schools, each in some phase of restructuring, and their desperate efforts to respond to state and district accountability requirements tell us definitively why changing one school at a time will never work. Although their leaders have the best of intentions, these schools and innumerable others like them inevitably fail. Stories like these show us the folly of trying to solve the problem of poor performance by relying on planning protocols. They show how neither telling nor helping from a distance will ever work. They demonstrate that all the external pressure in the world only makes matters worse without building the capacity for school personnel to work together on focused instructional improvement.

The stories Stephens tells are concise yet full of insights. The lessons learned are crystal clear. There are many different ways schools fail; every school has its own particular history, tensions, and challenges that must be understood deeply if efforts at intervention are to succeed.

Stephens goes on to identify a core group of "foundational facts" and "central developmental dilemmas" faced by struggling schools, and shows how wave after wave of improvement efforts leaves these common elements unchanged. He then offers a threefold theory of action that takes us down a new path toward external intervention.

First, he recommends creating a developmental profile of each school, drawing on what we know about the stages of school improvement. Second, he urges staged implementation: helping schools make strategic decisions about improvement activities at every step, based on their developmental needs and capabilities. Third, schools must emphasize collaborative learning and problem solving to establish a foundation for instructional improvement.

This section of the book is especially effective because it allows us to compare three clearly described cases of systemic failure with an equally clear model aimed at correcting these problems. The result is a comprehensive vision of a developmental approach to intervention in struggling schools.

Stephens's solutions are compatible with much of my own work on internal school change, including the conclusions in my most recent book, *All Systems Go* (Thousand Oaks, CA: Corwin Press). In that book I make the case that "collective capacity" is essential for school and system change. What is needed is the focus on a small number of high priority instructional goals, such as literacy and numeracy (broadly defined); precision and specificity of practice; linkage to a strong and timely data base; and collaborative work both within and across schools. District-wide collaboration is especially effective. Using this approach, whole systems have accomplished substantial reform including major gains in student learning and achievement. These successes align with Stephens's main conclusions.

We now have a pretty clear and well-specified agenda for instructional improvement. For instructional improvement to occur, schools must engage in collaborative processes that build internal capacity and accountability, and must be nested in a system of purposeful support. There is no form of accountability more effective than when the individual and shared responsibility developed within a school is in turn supported by and interacting with other schools across the district and beyond.

Given the disheartening scope and persistence of school failure, given the increasing urgency and attention due to the topic as one of Arne Duncan's four pillars of reform, and given that under the current accountability system most schools will inevitably continue to fail, anyone contemplating school turnaround should first learn the lessons contained in this book.

—*Michael Fullan*
    Ontario Institute for Studies in Education, University of Toronto

The Instructional Improvement Crisis

There is an emerging crisis of school accountability in this country. It isn't the same crisis we faced a decade ago, when the national debate centered on testing and standards and the need to know schools' results. Instead, we're facing a new round of challenges: Having passed beyond the arguments about whether schools should be held accountable at all, we're trying to figure out what to do with the thousands of schools that aren't good enough. Included in this group are schools that are persistently dysfunctional, along with many others that truly have gotten better, but not with the speed demanded by federal regulations. For a host of reasons, these schools haven't converted the labels and sanctions imposed by states and districts under the No Child Left Behind Act into any dramatic leaps in student learning. They haven't capitalized on the new performance data available to them. The new crisis—the most recent in a long series of urgent calls for reform—centers on how to fix this underperformance.

This is, as many describe it, the civil rights issue of our generation. At its sharpest point, we're talking about what to do with the roughly five thousand chronically low-performing schools identified by Education Secretary Arne Duncan early in his tenure under the Obama administration. More broadly, we're talking about effecting lasting, sustained improvement in the thousands of additional schools that have been labeled

1

underperforming since 2001 and that have, for too many years, failed to lift their students into a full set of life options. This is a far-reaching problem, one that has spared neither city nor suburb. Left unsolved, the new crisis—the instructional improvement crisis, as it's more aptly understood—threatens to dismantle the decades-old movement toward accountability in public education. Unless it is approached and resolved in a far more thoughtful, deliberate way, we're left to accept that the aspirations of the hundreds of thousands of students who continue to attend the same low-performing schools will remain stunted.

This is a book about what's left undone after the first decade of the accountability movement. More specifically, it's about how little progress we've made in improving the educational outcomes of children in low-performing schools and how state intervention isn't working in the way that anyone hoped. Finally, it's about outlining a new orientation toward intervention in troubled schools—a developmental orientation that accounts for patterns of growth and change in school improvement, the dilemmas schools face as they navigate this trajectory, and the overarching need to overcome the isolation and confusion that so often thwart their efforts to move forward.

Time and again, state accountability and intervention in low-performing schools collides with the realities of the established culture and relationships in these schools. In some cases, this collision appears to bring about promising new practices or at least helps set in place the conditions that might lead to sustained improvement. In others, the collision is like a powerful wave rolling to its quiet conclusion on a long beach. After the wave's energy is dissipated, the beach remains unchanged; the low-performing school retains its most persistent, limiting features. One could call this dysfunction at the school level, but the label is simply too facile to do anyone any good. We need to understand better what happens in low-performing schools in the throes of intervention, and then we need to get better at making intervention work.

Since No Child Left Behind became law, states have been compelled to build testing and accountability systems that over the last few years have pointed an increasingly bright light at the problems of chronically underperforming schools. In fact, there is no state in which lawmakers, board members, education officials, and teachers are not confronting the complex challenge of helping these failing schools get better.[1] So far, there has been no universal remedy for this chronic low performance; far to the contrary, the problem of persistently low performance in a significant segment of America's schools is a crisis now well at hand.

To illustrate this point, in 2007 the *New York Times* reported that 11 percent of the country's schools already possessed some label as underperforming. It predicted that should current trends prevail, this ratio stood only to increase. By 2009, not a single state in the nation had an underperforming school rate lower than 11 percent, and in some states, the rate was approaching 50 percent. In some states, more than a quarter of school districts faced similar labels, sanctions, and improvement regimens.[2]

The problem of failing schools is hardly new. But the problem of large numbers of failing schools facing intervention, takeover, and reconstitution—without any evidence that states can make these extreme strategies work—is becoming the leading edge of the accountability movement. Frankly, the risks at this moment are profound: The momentum of an educational movement many decades in the making stands to lose its legitimacy—and might just evaporate. And many educators are asking why it shouldn't, since so many schools are entering the terminal stages of the accountability system and so many states are either out of cash for these schools or just out of ideas altogether.

No Child Left Behind (NCLB) and all its variant state systems for testing, accountability, and intervention have far outstripped any collective knowledge about how low-performing schools get better. In state after state, sets of chronically low-performing schools are nearing the end point of the accountability system. These schools have exhausted their state's attempts at intervention and have used up the limited number of years they were afforded for significant growth. In ever larger numbers, they now face reconstitution, takeover, or enforced "charterization." These are, however, triggers no one seems to want to pull, mainly because so little evidence suggests that these extreme strategies will yield better outcomes than the schools' own efforts.

From a policy perspective, there aren't a lot of great options right now. Giving up certainly isn't one of them; the children, and what they represent for our future, are just too important. We've made it only so far by applying theories about incentives, signals, and the possibility of inducing better motivations among teachers through fear and shame. Dishing out more of the same is not going to work. For the next generation of intervention, we need better information about what makes improvement so challenging in low-performing schools.

President Obama and a New Round of Reform

Less than a year into his administration, President Obama and Education Secretary Arne Duncan began to show their cards on all these issues, making clear that they favor an approach both solidly rooted in the accountability reforms of the previous ten years and even more ambitious in its willingness to confront what was left untouched by NCLB. Duncan signaled in his early speeches that federal education dollars would be apportioned to various entities: (1) the states willing to connect test scores and teacher performance, (2) efforts to describe a new set of "internationally benchmarked standards," and (3) public-private solutions to the challenge of improving the nation's lowest-performing schools. These goals are all best read as extensions of NCLB, as an even more muscular form of the same policies. They are expressions of a nonpartisan, eclectic, and pragmatic view of the problems of modern education, and they are most striking in the way they advance the same agenda. The toolkit has been enhanced—we're seeing screwdrivers replaced by power drivers—but the basic design of the project remains unaltered.

As the Department of Education launches its Race to the Top program, with at least $3 billion dollars to be dispensed at Duncan's discretion, there's more burnishing going on than anything else. The earlier decade's charge to place a highly qualified teacher in every classroom has been replaced by the desire to document the teacher's effects on student learning. The ten-year-old rush toward state standards may soon be replaced by the creation of national standards, with $350 million already set aside to begin work on a national standards-based assessment system.

With respect to the future of the country's most resistant low-performing schools, Obama and Duncan have described several more options than those conceived under the Bush administration—mostly in the form of private takeovers of failing public schools or school closings. To set this tone, Duncan publicly highlighted his own experience as Chicago's superintendent in closing a handful of failing schools. He also pointed to the aggressive posture of the Los Angeles Green Dot Charter Schools, an expanding charter organization that has conducted something akin to hostile acquisitions of Los Angeles Unified School District schools all over the city, as a model of how takeovers might work. The secretary has also discussed the creation of takeover teams for low-performing schools, an option in which a new principal and new teachers can apply for a one-year planning grant and then step into a failing school as the replacements for the former staff.

For the most part, the examples cited by the federal government, however limited they are in number, have apparently benefited the students and families affected by these decisions, but the question of scale seems as obvious and pressing as in any past attempt to fix failing schools. Setting aside the rather large question of political will, the thoughtful observer is left wondering just where the capacity to seize and remake thousands of schools will come from. Where is the expertise? Where are all the new principals and their teaching staffs?

Green Dot Charter Schools are not the only innovative organizations on the field at this moment, and the Obama administration is clearly paying attention to all the interesting experiments. There is probably none so controversial as Michelle Rhee, a Washington, D.C., school superintendent who dared to take on her central office, her principals, and teacher tenure in the first, astonishing years of her superintendency. As she makes what may be the nation's first large-scale run at tenure by offering teachers an option to exchange their protections during a one-year period for higher ongoing pay, other systems are charging toward charter schools. In early 2009, Philadelphia resolved to shift the management of thirty-five of its schools to charter companies, and Los Angeles ceded another fifty. In Massachusetts, where the schools described in this book are located, recent legislation related to the improvement of persistently low-performing schools allows for the doubling of the number of charter schools permitted within a single city and points toward "conversion"—either with or without a partnering entity—as the newest nostrum for failing schools.

All of these approaches—Race to the Top, tenure reform, charterization, school closure, and conversion partnerships—are closely aligned. Together, they reflect a willingness to move beyond traditional school districts to find solutions in the private sector. In the growing intolerance for the historical protections enjoyed by unsuccessful teachers, one can see the Obama administration looking for a back door into improvements in the classroom. This is an end run around the dozens of laws, labor agreements, traditions, and other habits that have so effectively sheltered instruction from so many reforms.

Intervention for the "Average" Struggling School

It would be wrong to read this book as a critique of any of the work going on in these and other areas of school reform, like charter and pilot schools, superintendent's districts, small schools, changes to teachers' evaluation, tenure reform, or pay-for-performance schemes. These are all important policy levers that might eventually make real differences for low-performing schools—especially if they're employed with an insider's knowledge of what goes on in these schools. But it is not yet clear whether they will have any effect at all on the culture they are trying to change.

Take a look at what's going on as teachers unions enter the KIPP (the national Knowledge Is Power Program) charter schools: they're right back to the same fights about teacher autonomy and overtime that engage everyone else.[3] Even if KIPP or Green Dot or some other group took over every low-performing school in the country, the same problems are likely to reappear. Similarly, new policy—like the Race to the Top regulations requiring explicit links between teacher and their students' test scores—is not enough to generate change on its own. If you want to predict how teachers will respond to having their individual performance judged on the basis of test scores, just look at how they've mostly reacted to having their schools judged in this way. The coast is awfully long, and its sand banks remain equally resistant to the crashing waves.

Moreover, while the administration's road signs may be indicating the direction forward, it's not clear how much traffic they will direct. Most cities, towns, and states are not yet ready to slough off their lowest-performing schools and are not much further along in their understanding of how to help these schools than they were ten years ago. In the short term, the basic organization of schooling is simply not going to change in the majority of low-performing schools. Contractual protections are going nowhere. The one-teacher-per-classroom, one-principal-per-school formula is a well-settled matter. Experiments with charters, tenure, and everything else are marginal occurrences; in the main, schools and contracts and state educational laws will exist mostly as they have, and there is little that five billion dollars can do about this. Our school system, with all its variable outcomes, is a robust, hundred-year-old institution, and the pragmatic, thoughtful leader is well advised to understand the system we have, without being distracted by all the bright, flashing lights.

Consequently, in the vast majority of cases, we need to find a way to help low-performing schools in the context of the same basic organization: the same cadre of teachers, the same school buildings, the same budget limitations, the same basic number of instructional hours, the same class sizes, the same publishing companies and teaching materials, the same state laws, the same unions that define themselves as something somewhere between industrial trade union and professional organization, the same disconnect between universities and public schools, and the same systems of local political governance. And if all these things aren't likely to change, then neither is the culture of the average low-performing school. There is simply no way around getting into schools and doing the hard work of intervention.

For a new, smarter approach to intervention to succeed, policy makers have to be better attuned to the predictable outcomes in schools and the predictable hurdles. Schools are proving to be highly resilient in setting their own priorities. Teachers demonstrate a remarkable tenacity when they feel the best interests of their students are in jeopardy. The culture of the average American school, whether the school has been labeled as underperforming or not, can remain stable, even in the face of pretty significant shifts in policy. Even in a school with seven years of underperformance, it's easy to find the teachers willing to stare straight back at the state and say, We may be among your lowest-performing schools, but what are you going to do about it? Do you think you can do it any better? So far, the answer appears to be no.

A Closer Look at Intervention Schools

In this book, I argue for an approach to intervention that acknowledges that improvement is a developmental process. Struggling schools look very different and need very different kinds of support as they move from stage to stage. In order to support the thousands of ordinary, struggling schools effectively, we need to begin to understand each school deeply. It's in these schools and classrooms that teachers, principals, and superintendents grapple with the daily tasks of improvement. They dream up, push for, and sometimes curb all the big and little things that go into making a school a better place for children. These are the people who get the data from their schools' scores. They come up with the stories behind their own shortcomings, imagine the remedies, and most forcefully experience the emotional impact of the accountability system. We have to get to know their particular struggles and hopes and the patterns that make up the roadblocks they experience. To do so, we cannot backward-map the practices of the successful anomalies and then assume they have applications for everyone; this is about the details, about learning from the thousands of schools that haven't yet found a place on the map.

The three chapters that make up Part 1 of this book delve deeply into the experiences of three underperforming schools in Massachusetts:

Stoddard Middle School, Tanner K–8 School, and Connington Elementary School.[1] All are urban, complicated, and subject to a wide range of internal and external impulses. They are each at different points in the state's accountability system, from having just been labeled as a school "in need of improvement" (Tanner), to working for five years as a school "in corrective action" (Stoddard), to nearing the maximum permissible time for chronic underperformance as a school "in restructuring" (Connington). To the extent that all three schools try to use their performance data and to employ new strategies, their stories are straightforward enough. There's considerable nuance, though, in what each of these schools brings to the table, and it's in all these sticky details that the crisis of accountability is really made. Like so many low-performing schools across the country, all three schools are stuck in one way or another. This book is about what they're trying to do, what they can't seem to do, and what can be done to help.

Stoddard, Tanner, and Connington Schools are in various stages of learning how to use the data they're given. All three schools have identified new ideas to try and are making a variety of efforts to understand the effects of these new ideas on student learning. They are all trying to enact what was designed to be a rational, incremental improvement process. But pulling a bit at the threads of each school reveals that two of them have a very incomplete picture of what they could be doing. Moreover, the three schools have made little headway in their ability to focus on the quality of classroom teaching, and they face a series of hard trade-offs that seriously hamper even their most earnest efforts. Fundamentally, these problems are the consequence of each school's profound isolation. They experience great pressure, certainly, but they get no help. For the most part, they just don't know what to do over the course of years, and as a result, guesswork is endemic in their effort. If they get one thing right, they're just as apt to get the next one wrong.

These three schools from Massachusetts turn out to be fair representatives of what most states are have done in this area.[4] All through the first decade of the new century, low-performing schools in Massachusetts have experienced intervention as new mandates for data analysis, new templates for school improvement planning, and new requirements about monitoring. Districts in Massachusetts have invested in teacher coaching and student tracking systems, new instructional materials, and extended time programs, and all these things show up in the stories of the three schools in this book. For example, the intervention design of the Massachusetts schools isn't much different from New York's Schools Under Registration Review (SURR), California's Immediate Intervention/Underperforming School Program (II/USP), or Texas's requirements for the schools its rates as "academically unacceptable." All have involved performance targets, a new planning process, and some form of external assistance and monitoring. To be sure, there are variations, but the most elemental building blocks of school intervention have a national character to them. If a school isn't just closed or given over altogether to different management, then it has most likely been through similar intervention steps, no matter where the school is located.

What Is Going Wrong in Intervention Schools?

If most intervention hasn't been all that effective and if the same basic arrangements will exist in most schools in the near term, then it makes good sense to spend some time investigating the question of what hasn't worked—and why. Part 2 of the book begins by elaborating on this question, drawing on current research and previous case studies, which are presented in chapter 4. Chapter 5 outlines the key developmental dilemmas faced by low-performing schools and the stages at which improvement occurs; it also proposes a developmental profile for assessing the needs of struggling schools. Chapter 6 suggests a new set of operating principles for school intervention. Part 3, the conclusion, offers a glimpse of how the experience of the three schools discussed in the book might have been different if intervention had been staged developmentally.

Three Godzilla-size problems with the way we're currently going about intervention are described in more detail in chapter 4. First, as discussed above, intervention policy hasn't paid much attention to how the low-performing schools are different from one another. We've been banking so far that all schools can uniformly convert a few strategies—mostly data analysis, improvement planning, and program monitoring—into ongoing gains. We've been right that schools will use these strategies, but dead wrong in the assumption that the strategies have the same results. They don't, and for a lot of reasons. Nonetheless, for years, intervention has mostly consisted of these one-size-fits-all requirements, and except for various isolated experiments, the "mainstream" intervention school has no new tools to work with.

The second major problem is that the current architecture of intervention has done nothing to reset the foundational facts of these schools, that is, the basic conditions under which teaching and learning must occur. This is especially true of the professional isolation that plagues so many low-performing schools. In these institutions, after all, principals are notoriously overworked and have little control of their time, and teachers' workdays usually extend only a few minutes beyond their responsibilities as instructors. It's a system built to chronically hamper even in-school collegiality, and it's truly a hero's work to digest research, visit other schools, or thoughtfully and systematically observe new practices. It just doesn't happen. Isolation is a fundamental aspect of intervention schools—something, even, that we can safely predict. But so far, intervention hasn't done anything to change this.

The intervention schools portrayed in this book are indeed lonely places. When the principals and teachers in these schools chose improvement activities, they did so without access to any broad or helpful survey about what they could do, and without any help at all in tailoring their choices to the political, cultural, or intellectual terrain of their buildings. When they tried to implement these activities, they were all forced to deal single-handedly with pretty similar trade-offs about the politics of change, the reasons for their students' learning difficulties, the development of expertise among staff members, and the teachers' own sense about the privacy of their classrooms. When the principals decided to push hard for change or pull back to lower their teachers' anxiety, they did so without any help in understanding how these decisions would fit into a longer plan to improve. In fact, two of the schools had no long-term plan at all for the development of their organizations. They just piled on the data analysis, the collaborative groups, and the professional development in a single year—year after year—with no coherent developmental plan.

It's not that the schools were clueless in this work, but every day brought new challenges that carved away at the potential power of everything they were trying to do. Sometimes they made decisions that preserved this potential, but more often they didn't. The whole venture appeared to be a kind of gamble, mainly on the part of district leaders and intervention designers: with the sheer number of tough daily decisions these school faced—decisions that clearly affected the strategies the schools were trying to implement and the development of the schools' capacity—each of these three schools would most probably wind up in nearly the same situation it started out with.

The third big problem is that the intervention system reinforces a culture of compliance. For many schools, like the ones in this book, compliance becomes a source of comfort and consistently lessens the impulse toward more demanding efforts. New remedial programs, new instructional materials, and new meetings all may contribute to an air of urgency and seriousness—even if year after year, none of them has any effect on achievement. Compliance with state mandates becomes a kind of terminus for many schools, and in the absence of any ongoing guidance, faculty members may find a certain security in just doing what they are told. In such cases, the "compliance orientation" nearly eliminates the need for professional learning and problem solving, at great expense to the faculty's own sense of efficacy. The dilemma of this compliance orientation is described in more detail later in this introduction.

Given that intervention policy hasn't really sought to change the rule-book for most target schools—and probably won't anytime soon—it has pretty well ignored some of the basic realities these rules produce. For the three schools profiled in this book, the combination of a one-size-fits-all approach to intervention, an unaltered set of foundational facts, and the rewards of the compliance orientation was a brute they weren't likely to beat. For whatever effect poverty or city life had on these schools, one doesn't need to look much further than this combination to find the starting place for designing the next generation of intervention.

The Developmental Dilemmas Faced by Intervention Schools

As one takes a closer look at ordinary struggling schools, it becomes clear that intervention doesn't set in motion an inexorable march to high performance or, in some cases, even a crawl toward improvement. To the contrary, intervention appears to heighten the dilemmas that low-performing schools face, thereby making even more important the effectiveness and efficiency of the decisions they make. Intervention hasn't been a principal-proof or teacher-proof affair. It's been the opposite: it intensifies the balancing acts that schools must perform, and its potential is either upheld or undone by how schools approach these decisions. In their deep isolation, school leaders and their faculties are left to negotiate these dilemmas themselves, with a huge amount of idiosyncrasy as result.

Of course, life in public schools requires the constant management of dilemmas. This is the nature of work in a place where lots of people—from school boards and central offices to parents, students, and teachers—can exercise a great deal of influence on the organization. For example, principals have always had to deal with the tension between parents' demands and teachers' desire for professional autonomy. But the competing demands on school leaders intensify when the state ratchets up its pressure on a low-performing school, and this pressure exists, whether you're talking about principals, teachers, or anyone else in a leadership position. These intensified dilemmas, some familiar and some unique to schools in the throes of intervention, have been invisible in the national conversation about how to help. Nor have they been included in the design of any interventions. But they appear to be very real, and low-performing schools struggle mightily to resolve these dilemmas.

As this book unfolds, you will see that the dilemmas faced by Stoddard, Tanner, and Connington Schools—not data analysis or improvement planning per se—figure most centrally in what the schools are doing. In fact, none of the principals or teachers in the three schools had the luxury of viewing data analysis or improvement planning outside their implications for the tenuous balances maintained in other arenas of the school. Data analysis at Stoddard wasn't just about looking at the school's numbers; it was about maintaining the implicit social arrangements between a diverse group of teachers. Similarly, classroom visits at Tanner were not only about collecting data and providing feedback, but also about incursions into territory that teachers deeply felt was private. And taking on the Reading First grant at Connington wasn't simply a matter of considering the grant's merits and disadvantages, but was also a calculation about the staff's capacity at that time, the stability it might provide, and the need to comply with the state's short-term demands for new action.

In each of these decisions—and there were dozens of critical decisions at each school, stretching over a period of years—the school made an active attempt to balance competing interests, to reconcile contrary concerns. Some of these attempts may have been quite naive or lacked any connection to the generally limited bank of scholarly knowledge about turning around low-performing schools, but they were as well-considered as they could be in light of the confusion on the ground.

The point that emerges is that improvement in low-performing schools is not just a technical process. Nothing about the technical nature of state accountability and intervention reduces this point for the people who work in these kinds of schools. Instead, attempts at improvement are also efforts to resolve a set of critical dilemmas about the development of a complex organization.

Four of these developmental dilemmas, discussed at greater length in chapter 5, prove to be especially hard. First is the dilemma of attribution: the sustained internal battle over what exactly is leading to the failure of students. How to resolve the tension related to the root cause of student failure is the first dilemma confronted by the leaders in each of the three schools described in this book. These early conversations about attribution seemed only to exacerbate the sense of affront felt by teachers, and many staff members interpreted the school's new accountability status as an immediate challenge to their professional self-concept. For many teachers in these schools, the message from the state about inadequate performance and the insistence about taking personal responsibility felt something like unfair blame. They felt strongly that their professional work was impugned, and they then withdrew their support for any initiative they felt was connected to this blame. In at least Connington and Stoddard, this sense of teacher resentment, coupled with the need for the school to take immediate action, contributed to the staff's early alienation from the school's principal and teacher-leaders. These small leadership groups, charged with planning the school's turnaround without the consent of the staff, then banded together in opposition to the remainder of the faculty, creating divisions that would last for years to come. Rather than creating buy-in in these schools, the accountability crisis produced fission, and the impulse to take on the question of attribution as a precursor to all forms of change apparently accelerated this conflict.

In low-performing schools, including the three in this book, intervention also heightens the tension between centralized and distributed control—a second key dilemma. School leaders—whether they are the superintendent, the principal, teachers, or even the state, in the form of its interventions—must wrestle with the question of how to share power. The tension is made more pressing by the urgency of the school's position and the need to help disadvantaged children, and the tendency in these cases is obviously to take control, not to share it. In fact, to the extent that state accountability systems are predicated on the idea that teachers in low-performing schools need only to be properly motivated to produce improvement, the system assumes that removing control is in the best interest of students in these schools. At Connington School, for instance, the years of tight control evidently had some very negative consequences, both on the morale of the school's mostly new recruits and on their ability to exercise sufficient professional discretion in their classrooms. The control produced cynicism and fear, incurring negative repercussions for how thoughtfully and openly teachers went about their work.

Like the first dilemma, this second one relates to the larger idea that low-performing schools must grow their capacities. The short-term gains that may accompany tighter control in the early stages of accountability appear to bring few rewards later down the road. The understanding that school improvement occurs in stages, also discussed in chapter 5, provides a valuable framework for helping schools decide how to manage this and other dilemmas. In the early stages of the accountability crisis, for instance, is there more sense in building inclusion and goodwill by expanding the pool of leaders in the school, even if this expansion forces a delay in the serious examination of attribution, or even if the expansion is possible only by planning activities that don't immediately threaten the privacy of teachers' classrooms? The dilemma for school leaders is that teachers must eventually play the central role in solving the difficult problems of practice that hinder student learning. There is no teacher-proof program that will substitute for this work. Any approach requires an eye toward the future. In the early phases of reform, school leaders may need to consider some calculated risks related to sharing power and leadership in the short term. After all, problem solving, empiricism, and collaboration are not going to spring from ground that is poorly tended.

A third critical dilemma is how closely, and how quickly, schools should aim for substantive reforms in the classroom. Ultimately, they must marshal their resources to support the improvement of classroom teaching. This is the single most important activity in the organization and the most important lever for improving student achievement. In the short term, though, the battle over the sanctity of the classroom might need to be ceded.

In the same way that pressing early and hard on the question of attribution risks grave insult and instability, or taking immediate and tight control risks alienation and fear, there may be some benefit in focusing on constructing school programs outside the classroom as a way of homing in on quality. For instance, it may be helpful to concentrate staff efforts on developing a high-quality after-school program in which everyone has some say and which may have a quick if modest effect on student achievement. This can serve as a strategic precursor to paying attention to the quality of teaching in individual classrooms. For some low-performing schools, these kinds of low-stakes test cases can provide opportunities for the faculty to begin thinking together about defining and pursuing quality teaching. In the early stages of brushing up against state accountability, developing a system for rationally, systematically thinking about quality may count the most. The resolution to this and other dilemmas faced by low-performing schools, however, will vary according to the stage of a particular school's development.

Finally, teachers and administrators in low-performing schools grapple with the dilemma of compliance. As mentioned earlier in the introduction, for some people, compliance with external authority can become the central rationale for everything happening in the school. It can be the source of great resignation and even fatalism. In the schools described in this book, compliance was the central means for dismissing the validity of the state's efforts. Even more insidious, perhaps, was the complementary sense on the part of school leaders that compliance with external authority was—in and of itself—a reasonable strategy for solving the problem of low achievement. This willingness to focus on compliance in the short term has apparently curtailed the schools' later ability to support teachers' professional learning.

In effect, the emphasis on compliance in schools like these leads them to define the challenge of responding to state accountability as primarily technical. The successful response, this thinking goes, is measured in terms of the number of programs created, or students served, or meetings attended. In this model, it's the activity that counts, not the outcome. For people working learn. The single most important contribution that any school, low-performing or otherwise, can make to its students' learning will always come from its teachers' skills. In low-performing schools, the fundamental challenge is to help teachers learn new and more powerful teaching practices and to provide this support coherently and consistently. It's just not good enough to have a stellar teacher in one room, a mediocre one in the next, and a poor one down the hall. This is the case in nearly every school in the country, and changing this must be the bull's-eye for every school-improvement effort. The goal is excellent first teaching in every room in the school, day after day, through the entire year. This work of classroom-by-classroom improvement is slow and painstaking, and it only happens in schools whose culture, politics, and structure support it. At its heart, making every classroom work for every student is as much a challenge for a school's base of organizational knowledge as it is for its base of pedagogical knowledge.

Sadly, for schools like those in this book, intervention often isn't even successful in making excellent first teaching a goal that everyone shares. Those three Godzilla-size problems—the inflexibility schools face, their deep isolation, and the lure of the compliance-oriented response—just put too much in the way. If good first teaching is ever to become a common outcome of intervention, then a new set of principles is in order. These new ideas must gird a wholly different approach, one that at least starts by acknowledging what schools are really like and that provides timely, well-targeted support that helps schools and the people in them develop the capacity for change.

Part 1

Struggling Schools:
Three Case Studies

1

Stoddard School:
Five Years in Intervention

I n 2002, Massachusetts made its first set of public determinations about the handful of schools that had not satisfied the Adequate Yearly Progress (AYP) requirements for any year in which the state had used test data for school accountability. Stoddard Middle School in Harborview was one of these schools. Located in the waning seaport city of Harborview, the school was filled with the children of immigrants— from El Salvador and Colombia more recently and, earlier on, from Portugal, Italy, and Greece. Originally a center of New England commerce and shipbuilding, Harborview had entered a prolonged period of economic contraction, and its schools, though all recently rebuilt by the state, had for a generation been producing only meager results. Shortly after it was designated as an underperforming school, a team of teachers attended a three-day summer training session on performance improvement mapping (PIM), a detailed school-planning protocol that was the centerpiece of the Massachusetts Department of Education's intervention in struggling schools.

The PIM process is a series of detailed planning steps designed to help a school rigorously examine its own data. While PIM was in use in schools, it was meant to provoke an honest, internal reflection on the causes of poor performance and to lead to a thorough description of the student learning goals for the coming two-year cycle. At its core, PIM was to help schools identify teaching strategies that would lead to these changes in student performance.

As with any organizational change process, the members of the Stoddard PIM team encountered a variety of challenges in completing their performance improvement map. Some of these challenges were technical and related to the explicit planning steps outlined by the Department of Education. Other challenges were implicit in the task of leading the PIM process: team members were forced to wrestle with issues of leadership, change theory, institutional structures, and staff politics as unforeseen companions to the technical steps of PIM. This chapter tells these two stories—both the technical, explicit steps the team completed as part of PIM, and the implicit, unavoidable work that seemed to accompany the formal steps of the process.

The First Performance Improvement Mapping Plan

By March 2003, the handful of teachers asked to participate in the development of Stoddard's PIM had completed a draft of each of its sections and were prepared to bring the document to the school's instructional leadership team for review. For the PIM team members, the completion of this first stage of the PIM cycle brought mixed emotions. To Janice Medeiros, an English teacher at the school, the creation of the first draft of the performance improvement map was overlong and without context.[1] As a result, the team lacked an early understanding of what the DOE was requiring of them. "I think, going through the training, I was very overwhelmed, because it just seemed like we had all this work to do. It was three days of training. . . . . I'm still overwhelmed with the whole process. It just seemed very intricate, and there's so many pieces to it that all have to fit together." Stoddard's principal, Ken Schumer, himself new to the school and a longtime music specialist in the city of Harborview, described the work at this stage as laborious: "I find it seems like we get going on the PIM process, and we write goals that are extremely . . . extensive . . . I'd like to see it maybe streamlined a little bit . . . And not to say, torn up and thrown out, but just simplified a little bit."

In fact, the PIM team members were repeatedly overwhelmed by the complexity of drafting the PIM protocol as they took on the subsequent components of planning. In particular, the data-analysis portion of PIM proved to be especially challenging. "Basically, we've done so much, and there's still so much to do," said Scott Moraes, an untenured math teacher and one of the two teachers who, independent of the team, did most of the initial writing. He had been asked whether the group had enough time to study all the data it had access to. "When I say, 'Hopefully [we get to continue data analysis] with the PIM team,' . . . I use the term 'hopefully' in the sense that, if time permits. I mean, there is just so much."

This lack of sufficient time for data analysis was apparently compounded by the team's paper-and-pencil approach to studying student outcomes. Sara Tannen recalled joining Stoddard's staff that year as the school librarian and witnessing these early efforts to analyze test scores: "Mr. Canter, the principal at the time, let Moraes and longtime English teacher Jessica Jacques off for the last two periods of the day to work on writing this plan. And I just offered to go over and help them, and I just looked at what they were doing. They had stacks of papers everywhere. There was no organization to it. And I said, 'Why isn't this on a computer?'"

Jacques, the teacher who worked with Moraes on a first pass at the data, went further: "[It was] a little overwhelming to notice how much data was actually available, and initially thinking we had to . . . become very familiar with every bit of it. But obviously, as we sifted through it, and as the training continued, we were able to find which documents we wanted to target—and which of that big box of information would be most helpful." Though their inspection of the school's quantitative data was difficult for reasons related to time, experience, and technology, PIM team members' initial frustration wasn't limited to these problems. The educators also described their frustration with the number of steps in the process, including the student learning objectives and the instructional learning objectives required for each major strategy the school elects to pursue. And especially vexing was the DOE's dictate that PIM not mention in any way the range of demographic features in the student body, although the Stoddard faculty had used these features for years to explain the school's poor performance on standardized tests.

A Ruckus About Root Causes

A conventional assumption about reform in low-performing schools is that substantive organizational and instructional change requires a shift in teachers' thinking about what makes students fail. For some observers, like Jennifer O'Day, faculty in poorly performing schools simply do not or cannot apply serious professional introspection to their responsibilities for student learning outcomes.[2] By all accounts, the teachers and administrators at Stoddard were forced to grapple with this very notion about school change; in fact, PIM required that they take this notion head-on.

For example, one of the greatest challenges was changing the teachers' ingrained viewpoint on certain root causes. "It was absolutely off the table," said Jacques, describing the department's prohibition against discussing students' home lives as the school identified root causes in the first stages of PIM. "So, I understand that you need to engage students, and I understand you have to change practices in order to do that. But, still there are some very real things on a large scale that happen outside of the building that are distracting for students. And there's no structure. It certainly is a variable in all of this and how well they score . . . So why not in the demographics? Why can't they look at that? Because they can't fix it?"

"It was kind of hard to swallow it a few times," complained Tannen, "because there were root causes that [were] obvious and identified, and the DOE says no, that's not a root cause. You know, we cannot do that." Tannen was referring to the conversations about factors the team considered detrimental to students' opportunities to learn: poverty, lack of parental participation and support, violence and bullying in the community, home languages other than English, and inadequate academic preparation during students' preschool years. For the PIM team members, each of whom considered themselves among the school's most active leaders, the shock of this shift in thinking was profound. What was the most difficult, the department's rejection of the reasoning about poor student outcomes seemed to propel the teachers only toward self-blame. Even eighteen months after the announcement that Stoddard was an underperforming school, to P. T. Coelho, the plan facilitator, the requirement to look internally for root causes was an unfair demand: you were either realistic about the real-world challenges that affected kids at Stoddard, or you necessarily leveled unfair criticism at a dedicated faculty. "We were declared underperforming, so you can't [talk about demographics]. You know, [the designation] is not right for the kids. It's not right for us. There's nothing wrong with the teachers here, so the teachers all felt that, at first, 'It must be me. I must be a sucky teacher.' Until we got to the point where we said, 'You know, if you were working in Newton or Wellesley, you'd be just as good as those people. It's just that they're not having kids under, you know, 220.[3] That's the bottom line. You're not any worse. You're probably better because you can handle 90 percent of the discipline problems that are thrown at you, and you're doing some teaching, too.'" To Coelho, who exercised great influence over the completion of the performance improvement map, Stoddard's problems had nothing to do with the school's quality; the entire matter of the school's performance was a function of location.

Several events in the drafting of Stoddard's first PIM plan diminished many teachers' early resentment about the department's prohibition on talk about students. First, the team's plan was rejected repeatedly by DOE staff because it failed to satisfy the requirement that root causes be firmly under the control of school staff. Months later, to the chagrin of the staff, a department investigator issued a public report excoriating the school for its refusal to accept responsibility for the outcomes it produced. Principal Ken Schumer described how the staff eventually turned its anger around:

> The [teachers'] idea was to blame the elementary school for ill preparation. But then I said to them, "Look, if we blame the elementary schools, who do you

think the high school's going to blame? They'll be blaming us for kids coming unprepared."

So . . . they were in denial as to the cause. When . . . we read [the fact-finding report], people had to say, "Yeah, that's the truth. There are some pockets of bad teaching going on. The corridors are a mess. There's no civility in the building. Language is raw and rough. Teachers don't come out of their classrooms. They lock the doors . . . They're afraid of supervision."

Though many teachers on the PIM team continued to express some doubt about the DOE's strict limit on the discussion of root causes external to the school—Coelho's perception about Stoddard's students being the real difference between the school and its higher-performing counterparts represents this perspective—the PIM work did have some effect. At least among the members of the planning team, there was a willingness to concentrate on what occurred within the school's doors. And for teachers unable or unwilling to make this shift in thinking, there was at least the threat of consequences from within the district. "Statements were made not only from the superintendent, but from our union, that if you didn't want to follow these steps, 'We'll find you another position,'" recalled Jacques, who viewed this possible penalty as a kind of trump card. Under this threat, it was of little consequence that teachers at Stoddard understood the department's rationale for limiting discussion about students; it was simply something that had to be done. "People didn't have a choice," said Jacques. "I think they need [this threat of consequences] to conform to the new methods of teaching."

In fact, all these threats—from the union, the district, or the state—would eventually become cover for much of the PIM team's actions. In a sense, the DOE's ultimatum became the primary operating model for the team as it pushed for change. It was as if the team were saying, "These things may not make any sense to us, either, but there's little point in resisting." In the words of one Stoddard teacher, "Let's just get it done."

Developing the PIM Team

Early in the PIM process, Stoddard's key figure—whether it was the former principal or Ken Schumer—conceived of PIM as an opportunity to generate interest, buy-in, and cooperation from the faculty. As Jacques described, she was approached by Schumer to complement the existing team for reasons that she understood as expressly political. "The original PIM team was developed two years ago, but I was asked to be on by the current principal. Apparently, he was striving to have one person representing each team within the building. And there are six academic teams, so that's how [the recruitment] started." In addition to believing that they were selected to represent a section of the school, many PIM team members cited their attitude toward school change and their willingness to take on additional, unpaid responsibilities as reasons for their recruitment by the school's leaders.

By March 2003, the PIM team had several defining features. To begin, the team drew almost exclusively from the same teachers as those who had seats on the school's instructional leadership team. Of the seven teachers writing the PIM plan for the school, five were also members of the instructional leadership team. In effect, it was almost the same group of people.

Additionally, the work was relatively new for all team members. Four of the seven members—Schumer, Moraes, Tannen, and Medeiros— were all in either their first or their second year of work at Stoddard, a circumstance that each of them would later cite as an influence on their perspectives on data analysis, strategy selection, implementation, and monitoring. As Medeiros explained, "If it were me, [an older teacher] being asked to do this, how would I want to do it? Would I want to be told to do this, or asked [to do it]? . . . You know, people have techniques they use in their own classrooms, some that are successful that I might not use. So, [I try] to look at all those different aspects in writing the plan." Even for Stoddard veterans on the PIM team, this was new work: Coelho was just months into his role as PIM facilitator, and not one of the teachers had ever played a role in the development of the school's previous improvement plans.

The PIM team had a decided bias in subject-area orientation. Schumer, Coelho, and Aiden Canter, Stoddard's former principal, had been careful to recruit teachers in equal numbers for the math and English departments, but no teachers represented the school's science, social studies, or elective departments.

Finally, about six months into the PIM work, the group that I encountered in March already represented a fairly high level of turnover: Schumer had just brought in Medeiros to replace an earlier recruit who had withdrawn from the team. Tannen, the librarian, had joined the team only when she happened to come upon Moraes and Jacques struggling with reams of paper reports. Coelho was appointed to the just-created facilitator's role in December, and Schumer, only nine weeks into his entry as principal, was also new. Of the seven, only three members had been a part if the DOE's three-day training session the previous summer.

It's significant as well that both the principal and the PIM facilitator conceived of their role in PIM in the context of their other responsibilities. Schumer explained, "We have discipline issues, we have medical issues, we have staff issues, we even have to hire the subs. I try to leave before 3:30 so I can get to the administration building with the mail. That's a long day, and there's a lot of things going on." Coelho could relate to this. Between PIM meetings, and even when I met with him on several occasions, he was called on to deliver copy paper to the office, fix a broken computer for a teacher, and track down a telephone missing at another school. As Schumer and Coelho described it, delegation wasn't just something a good leader did; it was a matter of absolute necessity. However, in the favor-based economy of the Stoddard, the two saw that there was greater gain in taking care of the little details than there was in guiding the creation of the school's plan. Paradoxically, the Schumer and Coelho saw that their contribution was better made by staying out of the way—even if this meant giving up control of the substance of the PIM team's work. The net effect of these leadership decisions—whether they're made pragmatically or philosophically—was that the plan's substance was created mainly by the teachers on the PIM team.

Perceptions of the Department of Education

Since the summer of 2002, when five members of the Stoddard faculty attended a three-day training for underperforming schools, the PIM team had many interactions with the Department of Education. In fact, every member of the school's planning team realized that PIM was itself very new to the department and that the school was unfairly disadvantaged because the department was creating and implementing the process in nearly simultaneous fashion. In part, reasoned the PIM team members, the back-and-forth between the DOE and the school—the series of PIM plan submissions and rejections—during the first half of the 2002–2003 school year was a function of early disagreements about how to describe the root causes of the school's problems. But there were just as many frustrations for the team members in what they perceived as the number of changes to the process itself. "DOE revision lasted . . . I can't give you the measurement in months, but certainly it didn't let up until the plan was finally accepted," said Jacques. "Because it did get to be kind of a banging-your-head-against-the wall kind of thing. It kept coming back needing revision and wasn't going to be accepted. This had to be done, and this had to be tweaked."

By the time the plan was accepted midyear, a certain sense of cynicism had drifted into the PIM team's feelings about the DOE. First, in the face of multiple redactions to the process itself, the team members apparently had difficulty in maintaining their view of the DOE as a useful source of expertise and as a munificent partner in the school's improvement. Second, and more significant, the team members generally believed that the rejections of their plans had only to do with wording and not with any major issue of substance. "[The PIM plan] kind of felt phony," Jacques continued, "in that we had to think about things that we wanted to do and word them in a certain way. What was the point of that? There were bigger things going on other than that, but, obviously, that needed to be done in order to have the document accepted." Over time, Jacques explained, the team developed a conception of the PIM plan as a type of "formula," in which old ideas could pass for new thinking, just as long as the formulation appeased the department's need for proof of introspection and ownership.

Sara Tannen elaborated: "I think [the team] identified that students don't have the basic math skills needed to succeed in the Connected

Math Program. All right, that was a root cause. Now, we couldn't say that parents can't help the kids with their homework. You couldn't say that was a root cause. So, you identify it [a different] way." In this case, the team wrote that students lacked basic math skills, and then it decided that the school's math periods needed to be expanded from fifty-three minutes to sixty minutes to account for this deficiency. It's a question of how much this conversation represents a shift in the team's own conception of root causes and whether they developed their own "code" in the performance improvement map that threaded the needle between the DOE's requirements and the school's prevailing belief that the source of students' learning problems were located firmly outside the school. Indeed, Scott Moraes said, PIM never radically departed from what the school had always done. "There is nothing in there that is a complete one-eighty of teaching practice. It's something that [teachers] just need to modify, certain things here and there." The danger in the thinking is self-evident: if the state's intervention is strictly about satisfying the terms of a formula—if it's entirely an act of compliance—then let's just find the words they like and get back to what we're doing.

Strategy Selection

As PIM progressed, team members were eventually asked to use the data to compile a set of strategies that they believed would alter instructional practices at the school and would improve student learning. In the parlance of the DOE, the team was first asked to translate its conclusions about the sources of students' weak performance on the Massachusetts Comprehensive Assessment System (MCAS) tests into a series of student learning objectives (SLOs)—concrete statements about the intended effects of instruction on students' abilities. From this point, the team was prompted to develop a complementary set of statements about changes to teaching practice, each statement meant to describe a desired end state for instruction in all classrooms. The progression from test data to root causes, and then from learning objectives to goals for changes in teaching, was conceived by the DOE as a series of closely linked, logical steps. Weaknesses in students' understanding were to be linked to deficiencies in teaching practice; teaching practice was to be affected by professional development, increased sources of data about instruction, and a heightened person-to-person accountability for teachers. On paper, one thing was supposed to link to the next.

Despite the stepwise progression in thinking that PIM represented, there was still considerable leeway for the Stoddard PIM team as it considered and selected the instructional strategies that eventually appeared in the final version of its plan. From December 2002 to March 2003, the team mulled its options. This selection process—how the team came to champion some changes while discarding others—represents another critical component of the team's decision making. Like its other decisions about leadership, team formation, or root causes, there was considerable room for team members to bring their preferences, concerns, and experiences to the crafting of the school's goals.

Inasmuch as the PIM team received no specific guidance from the DOE, the district, or any consultant about the effectiveness of any particular teaching strategy, this deliberation seems to have involved the identification of a few particular teaching strategies from the broadest possible pool of ideas. More accurately, the selection depended on what the team members themselves considered best practices—either from their own classroom repertoires, from their observing or talking to other teachers in the building, or from their knowledge on the current state of the art in teaching.

As the PIM team began to select a strategy, they devised an impromptu system for collecting their peers' ideas about what best practices at Stoddard looked like. Ted Moreira, a twenty-year veteran at Stoddard and the team's most senior member, described fundamentally an opportunity for collaboration: "I think by asking other teachers, getting them involved with one another, talking about it, looking at some of the results from some of the testing they did, is how we arrived at what we felt should be incorporated [in the PIM]." Tannen, who as the school librarian was frequently not assigned to classroom duties, saw her role in slightly different terms; to her, this was a time to collect as much information about teaching at Stoddard as possible. In effect, the PIM team became a sort of catch basin for collecting teachers' descriptions of their own teaching practices. "Because I didn't have a classroom, I could . . . make lots of contacts with people where other [team members] couldn't get together. I could do a lot of running around, gathering information where needed." More, perhaps, than drawing any obvious conclusions from the data about gaps in teaching at the school, this phase of PIM was founded on consultation with peers. Though teachers outside the team had at that point no access to the data provided to the team, these teachers were nevertheless the primary source of the teaching strategies that finally appeared in the school improvement plan.

Teachers involved in PIM also brought to the plan their own knowledge about the current state of the art in teaching. Scott Moraes talked about the popularity of cooperative learning as the driving force for including this language in the plan: "I guess one of the buzzwords that they have right now is this 'think, pair, share' mentality. And I really believe that in certain cases and certain units . . . students need to speak out to someone, to tell them what they've learned." In this case, and in many others, the strategies selected for the school's plan appear to have been drawn directly from the repertoires of the team itself.

Like other schools, Stoddard was also involved in professional development, and many of these efforts predated the arrival of the PIM intervention. In most cases, these preexisting strategies—some brand new, others that had involved at least some of the Stoddard staff in training—found their way into the performance improvement map. PIM, the team members explained, was not especially about discarding strategies the school or district had already adopted. "Sometimes, the textbooks were either being changed or had just been changed," said Jacques. "It was a good time to implement new classroom practices or strategies. I thought things worked out well in that respect." Cohumor was more exhaustive in his description of how PIM interfaced with the many initiatives that existed at the time of the state intervention. His list of initiatives was an amalgam of the school's own efforts combined with offerings from the Harborview central office and regional professional development. It included work with local consultants, offerings from regional centers, and commitments to several curriculum-oriented foundations. Though none of these initiatives were discontinued with the advent of PIM, only a few appeared in the plan. In areas where the formal plan omitted the school's own preexisting efforts, the school apparently retained its own informal plan. The members of the PIM team never considered whether their new improvement work was diluted by the school's past commitments; the new initiatives were just piled on with the old.

In other instances, PIM team members appeared to be acutely aware of the role of seniority at Stoddard—especially in light of the recent contractual disputes that had lent such an air of uncertainty and group allegiance to all the city's schools. This uncertain atmosphere apparently infiltrated the work of the PIM team as well, and several teachers responsible for selecting teaching strategies to include in the plan spoke of the importance of deferring to senior teachers' expertise. For some PIM team members, this deference to the experiences of senior teachers was more a function of their own recent arrival to the profession. "Other . . . PIM team [members] who had been here a longer time know more different techniques, like different ways they did things, or things that they used to do but didn't work," said Moraes. "Half of those things I had never heard of, because I was so new to being here and to teaching." Janice Medeiros, the young English language arts teacher who was a early participant in the PIM work, explained: "We have to work with these people, and so what makes me better than the next person to go in there and say, 'What are you doing? What are you doing with this?' At least that's the way I take it. John Rivihno has been here fifteen years. I would never go to John and [ask], 'Do you need help doing this? Are you doing this, or are you not doing it?'" For Medeiros, this desire to avoid presumption led to a less-confrontational approach to identifying instructional strategies for the improvement plan. "It was much more looking around the school and figuring out who's doing [good work]—even looking at people and saying, 'Okay, what do you do in your classroom that is effective?' And then just having some people come back with their ideas."

For other members of the team, their selection of key teaching goals was just another opportunity to include the broadest possible number of people in the plan and to engender a sense of ownership. Moraes envisioned the PIM team's role in a way that was explicitly about expanding support. In fact, the very writing of the plan was the primary means by which the team could gain support from the Stoddard staff and shed its early reputation as a "secret government." "We had to make sure that it was clear that we were working for them, and . . . [that] if they have any concerns, [we'd say,] 'You bring them back to us and we can look at that.'" One way that the PIM team could assure its peers that it was truly an inclusive and representative group was to include a broad range of teaching practices in the plan and to consider the wording of the plan in light of teachers' possible reactions. "There were certain practices that we know take place in the building all the time," explained Jacques. "So, we thought that if we looked at some of the most cutting-edge practices that were taking place in the building, be sure to implement them, but word it in such a way that the people [who] were doing it would continue to do it. But we didn't want to overwhelm those people who looked at it and found it to be something they hadn't quite [seen before]."

This notion that "cutting-edge" practices could be introduced to teachers more easily by couching the descriptions in more prosaic language also had appeal to Medeiros. She openly described the great caution employed by the PIM team in selecting strategies for the new plan; in her mind, there was no need to sabotage the plan by including instructional strategies that were unnecessarily challenging to her colleagues. "We did as much as possible to go outside and get people who were not on the PIM team to give feedback. 'Okay, what are you thinking?' And I think that was helpful, because now, everyone has a piece of it, and [can say to themselves] 'Oh, that's something I do anyway.' So, it might be a little bit easier. I think that we were really cautious of how others were going to feel. And even the contract issues in this going to be a problem or not? I think that we were really careful not to step over any boundaries."

As Stoddard team members described their thinking about how they selected the final set of teaching strategies for inclusion in the PIM plan, a well-considered process of editing apparently took place. For a number of reasons—either political, experiential, historical, or convenience-related—team members took an active role in deciding how to develop this particular section of the plan.

Self-Organization for PIM

The final draft of the performance improvement map was in reality the result of two concurrent processes. The first, described above, was the steps specifically prescribed by the Department of Education as necessary to the development of a new kind of improvement plan. Teachers at Stoddard were told explicitly what to think about, and in what order.

The second process, though, was not in any way defined; it consisted of how Stoddard organized itself for the PIM work. Aspects of this second process included the teachers' and administrators' early reactions to beginning PIM and how the team settled important questions about leadership, membership criteria, the degree of inclusion of the larger faculty, root causes, the DOE's intentions, and instructional strategies.

These less-well-defined components of PIM had a critical bearing on the content of the final plan and its implementation. Though not the only influences, these were the first critical decisions the school faced in this new work that the DOE considered the centerpiece of the school's turnaround. The plan was different because of these things, without any conscious deliberation about the effect of these decisions or, seemingly, even an awareness that important decisions were being made. Still, the school satisfied the terms of the state's intervention, and by March 2003, it had a final and approved version of the PIM plan.

The PIM plan for Stoddard School was a dense document. Made up primarily of tables, most of its thirty-seven pages defined a series of major goals, student learning objectives, instructional change objectives, timelines, required resources, individual and group responsibilities, and measures of implementation. It differed in structure from the school's past improvement plans in several key respects. First, the PIM plan required a level of data analysis well beyond that of past plans; the school had to draw from its data to theorize about the root causes of students' performance and to specify each of its actions steps. It could not rely on the anecdotal evidence that had informed its previous plans. Second, the PIM plan asked that the school describe very specifically the problems that led to the failure of past plans, and these problems had to be things over which the school staff had control. Third, strategies related to instructional and organizational improvement had to articulate what students and teachers would do differently when the strategy took effect and when specific individuals would be held responsible for its completion. Finally, the plan asked that the school identify additional sources of data about teaching and learning for the purpose of developing an ongoing and more frequent understanding of the plan's enactment.

New Data About Implementation

The final component of Stoddard's plan was the set of quantitative and qualitative indicators of the plan's implementation. These indicators represented a new type of data for the school; for the first time, staff members were measuring the extent to which the strategies in the PIM plan were put into practice by teachers throughout the school. The data might look at, for example, the number of teachers who had posted standards in their rooms or who used a particular convention to teach and assess student writing, as well as some sense about the quality of this implementation. The plan also identified a set of data about outcomes for students. For example, in the Stoddard plan, students were to receive feedback and scores on the district's quarterly writing assessment, and these scores were to be collected and analyzed by the PIM team to measure the effects of changes in teaching practice on student learning. It is significant that these data were to be collected more frequently than the MCAS data. Instead of relying on the annual information provided by the MCAS— information that comes four to six months after the date of testing—the school pledged, through its PIM plan, to devise new sources of data to systematize data collection, and to analyze the data more frequently.

These monitoring efforts entailed weekly meetings with Coelho, the facilitator; members of the PIM team; principal Ken Schumer; and district liaison Calvin Alvarado. The team's agendas reflected the group's purpose at this stage in the two-year planning process: the members were to have collected evidence about implementation prior to the meeting and were then to spend their meeting time poring over test results, agendas from teachers' meetings, and general, confidential data from the administrators' weekly review of teachers' lesson plans and systematic reviews of classroom instruction.

In practice, this phase of PIM proved the most difficult for Stoddard School. For the team members, the monitoring phase seemed to have exacerbated the dilemmas that they had experienced so acutely when they were recruited to join the team a year earlier. If it was difficult to explain to colleagues why they had agreed to become party to the DOE's intervention at Stoddard and why they felt they could lead their peers in a process of change, it felt nearly impossible to play an active role in monitoring their colleagues' professional practice. In fact, to some members of the team, the monitoring phase was one in which they had been placed uncomfortably between their peers and their supervisors; their roles were no longer clear, and they each sought unique explanations for how the process would work.

Fundamentally, the dilemma centers on the difference between being a colleague and being a supervisor. Janice Medeiros, the team's least senior member, saw her only viable role as a PIM monitor in terms of her own individual responsibility. "There's things [in the plan] that I feel responsible for, so I could probably tell you what's being done. But as far as really being able to go into the room and saying this person's doing this fantastic job, I don't feel like that is my place." Veteran teacher Ted Moreira viewed monitoring as distinctly divisive: "I would probably say about 30 percent [of teachers are] happy, maybe 70 percent unhappy. I think they feel that we're judging, and that's not really our role . . . People aren't as enthused about it, because the minute you mention it, they'll say, 'Oh, yeah, of course, it's that little clique." Scott Moraes places the conflict clearly on the collective-bargaining agreement and the common prohibition on teachers' taking on a supervisory role. "A lot of the teachers on the PIM team [never] felt comfortable saying we're going to monitor other teachers. Personally, as one of the building's union reps, I say to myself that it is conflict of interest. The PIM team said, 'Look, we will make sure that the plan is being implemented. We will do our best to make sure that the practices are going forth.' But clearly, there has to be some kind of a line drawn."

To manage this seemingly intractable dilemma, the team improvised some methods for learning about other teachers' responses to the plan and their compliance with its expectations. Primarily, the members eventually treated this stage of PIM as essentially informal. Gone was the relative precision represented by the PIM's earlier focus on data about all students and all classrooms; in its place was a system based on peer groups and random opportunities for developing impressions about their colleagues' classrooms. Sara Tannen described the system: "Leadership team members don't necessarily do [any monitoring], other than they watch out for their colleagues in a way. They say, 'Hey, . . . where's this?' or 'Where's that?'—sort of in an informal way." Moraes, the union rep, continued in this vein: "I think [that monitoring] has been a very informal process, where now we have so much to do. We're just realizing we've done a fairly decent job. Let's take the next step, and the next step is let's make sure we are keeping track of every single thing we do."

By Moraes's own count, there is an obligation to keep track of changes taking place in the school—but not a commensurate duty to take some form of action if these changes are not occurring. It's about interacting with colleagues during the school's already-established meeting times and documenting conversations between teachers. This informal approach to monitoring instruction at Stoddard represented only one of a number of the team's investigative methods that threaded the needle between egalitarianism and oversight.

As the monitoring role evolved for members of the PIM team, they employed several techniques that they believed would help them understand how the plan was going in classrooms around the school. To Mahivian, monitoring the improvement of the school was about asking questions of her peers. "'What's going on?'" she recalled asking a grade-level counterpart. "'How are things? What are you doing in math? Here's what I am doing.'" For her, this interaction among teachers, which was common already among teachers at Stoddard, was easier than any sort of inquiry related to PIM. "I really feel a great level of discomfort about going in and checking on somebody else—because I wouldn't want it done to me," Medeiros explained. Tannen came up with her own method of polling the few teachers she knew as a teacher new to Stoddard. "I would poll a couple teachers that I knew would be trying to get everything done [in the PIM plan]. And if they weren't doing it, then I'm assuming the rest of the people aren't doing it, either." Though her method was even less formal than this system of polling familiar colleagues, Jacques came to rely on her interactions in the faculty lunch room to gain knowledge about the implementation of the PIM plan. "I felt enthusiasm from the people who I see on a very irregular basis in the lunch room, [people] who were excited about hanging the 'hamburger' model in the room or modeling their writing like everyone else."[4]

At PIM team meetings, the group did examine the new sources of data identified in the plan as midpoint indicators of the plan's implementation. The group placed considerable emphasis on the minutes from monthly grade-level and subject-area teacher meetings, both as an indicator that the plan's content was being disseminated and as a rough gauge of the faculty's awareness about its responsibility to enact the plan. The PIM team also collected individual student success plans as an indicator of teachers' efforts to differentiate instruction for struggling students, examined students' responses on a quarterly writing assessment mandated by the Harborview District, and shared anecdotes about students' level of participation in the classes. The most important source of qualitative data, however, seemed to be the level of consensus achieved by the group about the status of a particular action item. Said Medeiros of the group's process: "We talk about how much is getting done and whether people think it's getting done. But unless you really go in and look for that kind of data—unless I show you that I am doing it . . . well, there needs to be some level of proof."

On this question of proof—especially about changes in teaching practice—the school's particular attitudes about leadership, supervision, and internal accountability appeared especially confounding. As they talked about monitoring the PIM plan, member after member eventually conceded that the task was essentially administrative and that the responsibility for its implementation ultimately lay with its formal leaders. Moreira explained that the principal, both vice principals, P. T. Coelho, and, sometimes, the curriculum directors were responsible for the walkthroughs. They looked for specific things on the PIM calendar. "For instance," said Coelho, "if I'm supposed to have open-response questions, hopefully, as they're coming in, they're seeing some of that up there. Or they're seeing a sample of the 'hamburger' model, which we use for writing samples, or vocabulary. That helps a great deal. I think teachers [are] being more effective, as far as following [the PIM plan], because they know they're sort of being watched." As a matter of practice, however, Medeiros's view of the "level of proof" required to have some objective understanding about as large an institution as Stoddard was revealing: "Walk-throughs [by administrators] happen every day. Maybe not walking through the classrooms, but at least in the corridors. And it's done in a friendly way, so it doesn't seem like they're coming in and saying, 'Where is this, where is that?' It's done more as a friendly visit, not coming in to find out what you're doing."

Of course, Schumer's thinking about walk-throughs by administrators—and what he did in practice—provided the foundation of this theoretical system of checks. If he and other administrators had systematically reviewed teacher practice and provided feedback about implementation both to teachers and to the PIM team, the plan's design would have been enacted—entirely independent of its ability to usher in a new style of teaching in every classroom in the school. As Schumer talked about the walk-throughs, though, it was clear that he was still experiencing the same demands on this time as those he experienced earlier in PIM. He still held to his personal view that leadership is more meaningful when it is inclusive: We have commitments to do a lot of things. We have to do evaluations and all those other things. I try to walk through the building as often as possible. Some days, I go through two or three times. Some days, I don't have an opportunity to go through. Yesterday, seventh period was my first chance to get through the building . . . And I wish I had more time to do that."

For Schumer, walk-throughs, when he could make it through the building, had a number of purposes. First, he gave priority to staff behavior that was patently objectionable. As in the case of a special education aide who he recently encountered showing an inappropriate movie to students, it was his job to make maintain safety, order, and acceptable conduct. Second, he looked for markers of the types of instruction valued in the PIM plan, such as particular seating arrangements, standards posted on the wall, a reproduction of the school's "hamburger" writing model, or a lesson plan book that is open on and the teacher's desk. "A lot of [your understanding] you get from walking through, just by walking through, when you see the work that's going on, and the next time you're going through on a different day and there's work going on. So your assumption is that there's work going on all the time." In response to a question about providing staff members with feedback based on his observations, Schumer admitted that this happened less than he would have liked. In essence, he described a system that was much like the informal contacts Tannen relied on to collect information about the implementation of the PIM plan; the system coupled random samples of classroom teaching with assumptions about the general state of teaching in the school. As an example of the challenges associated with both accurately knowing about teaching practice and changing it, Schumer's comments were emblematic of this stage of PIM: there was no time to be in every classroom with any real consistency, and there was no effective mechanism for supporting change even if he or the PIM team discerned something to be improved.

What Went Wrong at Stoddard School: Five Common Intervention Mistakes

From beginning to end, performance improvement mapping introduced Stoddard School—mainly in the form of its PIM team—to a range of new challenges and dilemmas. Some of these problems were inherent in the intervention, which was designed to make the school wrestle with issues related to root causes, gathering and monitoring data, and internal accountability. The intervention, in fact, supposed that these things were missing in underperforming schools. As the Stoddard teachers described their experiences, it was evident that challenges inherent in the design of PIM were not the only ones they faced and that they had to resolve a host of dilemmas unrelated to the technical features of the plan. This second set of tasks—the work that was implicit in the PIM intervention but that remained unnamed—is explored on the following pages.

Two key observations apply to Stoddard School's required adoption of the state's PIM process. On the one hand, Stoddard's work to complete the process—from the first year's analysis of data and identification of improvement strategies to the second year's emphasis on implementation and monitoring—represented an undiluted effort to satisfy the terms of the state's intervention. The final plan complied with each of the steps in PIM and, in concept, held some promise for resetting a dysfunctional culture and bringing focus to the school. On the other hand, PIM required that the leadership team—the first and only group in the school to have had any meaningful contact with the intervention in its first two years—consider and resolve a series of unwritten dilemmas. Schumer and Coelho had to structure the steps of PIM—and the leadership team's interaction with these steps—in light of their own personal views about leadership and the demands of their ever-increasing workload. Tannen and Medeiros saw their involvement with PIM in terms of their status as newcomers to the school and initiates to the field of education. Moraes considered the implications of PIM only with respect to its impact on the collective-bargaining agreement, and his views on this topic were influenced by a recently simmering relationship between the union and the Harborview District school committee.

Compliance Orientation

This sense of being caught in the middle was a common observation among members of the PIM team, and their adopted positions had various consequences for PIM. Most significant, the orientation of the leaders of Stoddard School—keep in mind that the membership of the PIM team and the school's instructional leadership team was nearly synchronous—was primarily one of compliance. Though this orientation maintained a certain stability within the school—it failed to challenge the teachers' widespread, cynical belief that the DOE was not an ally in Stoddard's struggles—it came with certain requirements. First, PIM team members appeared loath to question the quality of the school's past efforts. Members defended the quality of the staff and its professionalism and avoided discussing analyses or strategies that would question core instructional practices. For example, the team's discussion of school's math scores only resulted in three action items related to this subject: that the school would add seven minutes to math instruction, that teachers would supplement the Connected Math Program with basic skills instruction, and that teachers would begin using the program's math journal component. There was no discussion of the quality of the program's implementation; nor was there any concerted, systematic effort to understand the teachers' challenges with the type of instruction represented by the school's new math program.

The team members' compliance orientation, itself most probably a function of their attempts to resolve the emotional complications of participating in the state's intervention, appears to have contributed to their reliance on intermediate measures of progress. That is, every member of the team made frequent reference to the completion of a variety of midcourse steps in the PIM plan and seemed to view their completion mainly as evidence that they had complied with the DOE's requirements. For team members, the collection of the minutes from grade-level team meetings, and the appearance of PIM goals on these minutes, was evidence of the school's good-faith effort to satisfy the terms of the state's intervention. In this sense, there was little incentive to question the effect of these activities on the improvement of teaching and learning. The minutes were small ends unto themselves, and for a team that saw itself as mediators between two hostile camps, these gains seemed to satisfy the needs of both Stoddard teachers and the DOE. The terms of the PIM plan were satisfied, and teachers were asked only to document what they were already doing.

Lack of Proactive Thought

There was also a marked deficiency in the team's sense of responsibility for troubleshooting any problems that might arise or for any thoughtful adaptation of PIM to the particular needs of Stoddard School. Though such tasks are not technically part of their responsibilities as defined by the DOE, the school's leaders must reasonably function not only as intermediaries in the intervention, but also as proactive engineers concerned with the fit and actual effect of the plan on the school's core functions.

Nowhere did this oversight have a greater impact on the implementation of the plan than in the collection of information about classroom teaching. In the strictest sense, Stoddard did comply with the dictates of PIM when it wrote about school walk-throughs, peer observations, and the weekly review of lesson plans. In practice, though, neither the PIM team nor the principal considered that these practices would require a substantial dedication of time and resources and would require a new division of labor if they were to be completed.

Nor was there any conversation with the central office about how the principal's time should be used. For example, during this whole period, in the midst of the school's AYP crisis, Ken Schumer was still required to leave the building each day at 3:30 to deliver the school's mail to the central office.

Another important factor missing was any discussion of the PIM team members' lack of time for research, collaboration, or data collection. By the same token, the PIM plan supposed the massive delivery of specifically targeted professional development by teachers, consultants, and the central office, all of which would have required altering Harborview's traditional custom of offering professional development to staff without respect to schools' needs.

When considered strictly from the perspective of compliance, all these problems may have been an acceptable state of affairs. From the vantage point of troubleshooting a new and challenging process, the actions of the school's leaders were not likely to have effected significant change.

Politicization of Strategies

The team of Stoddard teachers and administrators responsible for PIM also described how their own sense of interpersonal dynamics and politics of the Stoddard staff influenced how they carried out prescribed PIM activities. That is, it affected how they described data, selected strategies, monitored the implementation of these strategies, and even described the "reality" of the school. No respondent from the first round of interviews was immune to this subjective influence. In fact, the team members most likely saw PIM as primarily political, though more with an eye to protecting the social equilibrium of the school than viewing politics as a necessary medium for change.

There is no more compelling case for how political the PIM work was for Stoddard leaders than in their deliberations about which teaching strategies to include in the plan. Even if the team had possessed the capacity to identify the strategies that research suggested would have the largest impact on student learning, the team members were not, by their own admission, aiming for this result. Rather, they sought out strategies that they believed would earn the endorsement of the school's most influential teachers. It wasn't that some promising but potentially controversial strategies were considered and discarded; instead, there was no process for considering strategies outside the school at all, and this was done for patently political reasons. Staff cohesion wasn't the goal of the PIM plan; the PIM plan was a means for staff cohesion. In effect, the politics of the school—at least as they were perceived by the PIM leaders—served as the primary filter for the strategies the school selected to pursue.

If the selection of strategy during PIM included nearly every style of instruction in the school at the time of the intervention, it also led PIM team members to emphasize that teachers need only "tweak" their practice a small amount to satisfy the terms of the plan. Often, the teachers on the PIM team spoke of the new initiatives named in the plan as repackaged versions of what the school had always done. The content of teacher meetings did not need to be changed, just documented; the journal-writing component of the new math program was essentially the same as the very few writing assignments that math teachers had always given; the new focus on problem solving was the same as older versions of cooperative learning. Chiefly as a means of softening the politics of change, action items that represented new effort were billed by PIM team members as "reworded" versions of familiar practices. And if teachers who were uninvolved in PIM heard that the new plan would require little of them, the combined effect of the team's careful consultation with Stoddard's faculty about strategies, and the insistence that the school merely step up its current efforts, might have played some role in this perception.

Professional Isolation

On a related point, it is also a significant consequence of Stoddard's internal organization—the way it organizes its time and people—that the PIM team remained isolated from all external sources of expertise about instruction, leadership, organizational change, and any other dimensions of the work they were asked to lead. Overall, there was a remarkable absence of any external influence in each stage of the intervention. PIM teachers were free—and in fact, required—to develop their own theories about these important subjects, absent the experience and wisdom of members of the central office, consultants, professional organizations, or educational researchers. With respect to implementation, a stage in which support from Harborview's central office might have been essential, there was very little understanding among central office administrators about the specifics of Stoddard's plan. And in a district with a long tradition of filing school improvement plans at the central office without any process for even reading them, this continued isolation may have unintentionally reinforced the traditional hands-off relationship between Stoddard and its central office. Put simply, if two years of PIM had so far not involved the central office in the affairs of the school in a new way, there was little reason to think that the school had a new level of support coming to it.

Perhaps the most important domain in which PIM team members needed to take action had to do with their ideas about how schools change. In the absence of any training about change theories, team members developed their own particular theories about how to alter teaching and learning. As a result, the processes that the team developed for such critical activities like professional development, walk-throughs, teacher collaboration, and collecting and analyzing data were all affected by these beliefs. Professional development continued to be a voluntary pursuit at the school; the school continued its relationships with consultants and community organizations with no new regard for the goals laid out in the plan, and the Harborview central office continued to approve in-service offerings provided by teachers to their peers with only a consideration for the preference of the teacher-providers. Walkthroughs were conceived of as an opportunity to provide moral support and build relationships; administrators continued to stand in hallways, offer polite observations about students and the school, and supervise students. PIM team members made informal polls of the teachers they knew as a measure of how much—and how well—a strategy was being implemented. Though the plan asked for very specific measures and required the identification of every individual responsible for implementing the plan, the actual process was quite different. And in every case, PIM team members talked about their own ideas of how to support change. In this sense, the rigor of PIM wasn't diluted exclusively by a lack of will or time, but by team members' own best intentions—by their own improvised theories of change.

Indirect Communication

In nearly every interview of the Stoddard PIM leaders, there appeared to be a prevailing belief in the power of the clarification of instructions. If teachers just understand clearly what the plan asked of them, they reasoned, then teachers of goodwill would respond and enact these changes. There was the unique and relatively isolated problem of resistors, the PIM leaders said, but most teachers just needed reminders about their responsibilities in order to implement that changes in their classrooms. In this vein, the Stoddard PIM team issued a long series of memos, calendars, and checklists to the school's teachers, each intended to clarify the details of the plan, and each a sincere effort to bridge the gulf between the expectations of the plan and the team's perception of classroom reality.

Thus, to inform teachers about their responsibilities, Stoddard relied almost exclusively on written communication rather than face-to-face communication or, as in many other districts, the type of coaching relationships that have been documented as leading to significant change for many teachers. The team's belief that the primary challenge at Stoddard was that teachers needed to be convinced to embrace their responsibilities was also significant: this outlook placed little emphasis on professional learning—the idea that teachers may not know how to implement certain changes to their practice and require support for their own learning. In listening to the PIM team members talk about "veteran resistors," one heard a belief that each faculty member already possessed the knowledge needed to enact the new math program or to effectively teach the critical-thinking skills fundamental to skillful writing. By this reasoning, any perceived lapse in implementation could have been attributed to the failure of teachers to employ these techniques, because of either some consideration of their own teaching experience or a willful, political resistance. Two years into PIM, no team member—including the principal of the school—could offer any thinking about the challenge of teachers' "resistance" other than to prepare stronger arguments or to find better means of motivation. In their eyes, this was not a question of targeted professional development, supervision, or some other form of support; improvement was only a question of will.

In effect, the preceding five common mistakes represented how the PIM members reconciled the requirements of the performance improvement map with their perceptions about a range of emotional needs, their own personal beliefs, the school's political imperatives, and their own skills. PIM was designed to challenge each of these things; in fact, its creators posited that change in these areas was a prerequisite to change in teaching and learning. Each of these five common mistakes, however, served as a filter for the activities detailed in PIM. One misguided or ineffective activity greatly informed other, more productive activities, and at least in the first two years of Stoddard's experience with PIM, it's remarkable how seamlessly the two sets of activities coexist. Teachers seem not even to know that any dilemmas related to enacting their improvement plan may dilute the effects of their labor.

2

Tanner School: One Year in Intervention

I n the early fall of 2007, Tanner K–8 Community School, in the small urban community of Hoover, Massachusetts, received some immensely disappointing news. Set only a few miles from a larger city, Tanner School was bordered by large two-family homes and quiet streets of mature oaks, and the school's teachers considered their students mostly suburban. Tanner hadn't experienced many of the difficulties of Hoover schools that were located closer to the city center, but this appeared to be changing. After years of watching other schools in the city struggle with their own designations as schools "in need of improvement," Tanner failed to meet its own Adequate Yearly Progress (AYP) goals for the last school year. Its Massachusetts Comprehensive Assessment System (MCAS) scores came back, and though still higher than other schools in Hoover, they simply weren't strong enough to satisfy the state's demand that Tanner students make steady, incremental gains from one school year to the next. In Principal Trisha Waighn's estimation, "We really didn't do horrible, but we're very flat. If we go up a little bit here, we go down a little bit there." Waighn shared the sentiment of the majority of her staff: she was in shock, struggling to explain this new phenomenon to herself and to her teachers, wondering how the news might be accepted by them, and figuring out what would come next. By November, the news about the school's failure to meet its AYP target was only weeks old and the next round of testing would begin in three months. For the principal and her staff, there was little time to get it right.

Tanner, in its first year of contending with a negative accountability status, was a very different school from Stoddard. At Stoddard, the teachers were engaged with performance improvement mapping (PIM), an elaborate series of planning steps that focused the attention of their leadership team on the analysis of the school's data, the development of strategies specific to this data, and the monitoring of the implementation of these strategies. PIM was the centerpiece of schools' obligations to the state with respect to students' weak achievement. There, the members of Stoddard's PIM team struggled to reconcile the long series of very involved steps that PIM required of them with another set of deeply felt, but unofficial imperatives. These two sets of incongruent tasks—the explicit and the implicit activities of the PIM intervention—existed together only in great discomfort, but, at a minimum, the school did have a formal process through which it could respond to state accountability requirements.

At Tanner School, no such formal process related to the school's AYP status existed. In 2007, nearly four years after Stoddard had been wrestling with PIM, the state's decision to discontinue PIM was two years past. Tanner had just been tagged as underperforming for the first time, and so its response to its inadequate test scores was mostly its own to create. There were now no formal requirements related to data analysis, or planning, to strategy selection or monitoring; Tanner's only obligation was to the Hoover school district and to the plan that Hoover submitted to the state in response to its own entry the district's own "corrective action" status. Because these accountability requirements were so distinct for Tanner, very few of Stoddard's benchmark experiences, such as the PIM team's agonizing about how to collect data on classroom teaching, applied to Tanner. Its response to state accountability, then, necessarily proceeded differently from that of Stoddard.

In some ways, however, the two schools had common reactions. Tanner shared with Stoddard the intense and painful emotional reactions of being declared an underperforming school. Moreover, both schools similarly conceived of their dilemma as fundamentally connected to the poverty of their students.

But beyond these points, the tales diverge considerably. Because Tanner experienced no direct intervention by the state and no work that was distinctly new to the school, Tanner's response to its AYP crisis is best understood in relation to what it had been trying to accomplish for the last several years. Just as important, Tanner's connection to Hoover's central office was much like Stoddard's connection to the state. For Tanner, Hoover's superintendent was the authority to which the school had to bend, and he and his administrative team more naturally figured into the school's narrative. And in contrast to the tensions of the explicit and implicit activities of PIM at Stoddard, Tanner's central conflict apparently existed between two poles: the school and the district had a strong tendency both to consider change entirely a function of compliance and to conceive of change as something intrinsically linked to teachers' professional learning. These competing forces—one about telling teachers what to do, and the other about helping them do it—are shot through Tanner's story.

Reactions to Tanner's Accountability Status

To speak with any member of the Tanner faculty, one heard a nearly universal sense of Tanner's history: this small school in a reasonably affluent neighborhood had undergone a dramatic shift in the composition of its student body in the previous three years. Moreover, the school's new "in need of improvement" status sat incompatibly with the widely held view that Tanner was a haven from the plague of urban problems faced by its counterparts in other parts of the city. Yvette Bennett, Tanner's assistant principal and a thirty-year veteran in Hoover's public schools, represented the staff's sentiment in this way: "In other years, [the teachers] were feeling pretty elite. You know, that we were pretty special over here and we don't have those kinds of problems that they have in the other schools. And now all of a sudden, this being the first year [of not meeting the school's target], it's kind of hitting them that, yes, we do have a lot of those problems here."

Bobby Manopoulos was born in Hoover, coached boys' basketball for more years than he could remember, and was intimately familiar with the city's most troubled youth. He was the attendance officer for Tanner and four other Hoover schools, and before 2006, he couldn't remember ever being called to Tanner to assist with the types of discipline- and truancy-related problems he'd seen recently. "I think the drop in our test scores is directly related to the student population we serve," he said. "And I say this not coldly . . . There are a lot of families who may be single parents, parents working or who have other issues that prohibit them from helping their children be focused on schoolwork . . . I don't want to say it fits the stereotype, but a school doesn't change the way Tanner has changed with the student population, and then their test scores drop the way it's been documented, and the faculty not see any correlation between the two."

Another teacher was equally exact in his understanding of this connection: "Is it the school's fault? Is it that we're an underperforming school and we're bad at what we do? Or is it we're dealing with something else, that we're doing pretty darned well when we've gotten a lot more challenging kids?" This was the view held by many Tanner teachers: that after three years of consistent shifts in the demographics of the student body, the inevitable finally came to pass. In their view, there is only so much a good faculty can do in the face of such difficulties.

"The kids who have hopes, dreams, aspirations and want to go somewhere," explained Johnna Fitzgerald, a seventh- and eighth-grade social studies teacher, "there aren't enough kids for them to form their own clique of highly motivated, school-oriented kids. We haven't seen that in four or five years, that learning is valued and it's important and it's worthwhile. This year's senior class at Hoover High is the last group [that had this level of motivation]. We always say it's the best group we've had."

The discouragement among Tanner's staff was obvious. But although the staff generally agreed that the changes in the neighborhood had much bearing on the school's changed accountability status, the teachers had varied ideas about what else was going on. After all, schools are complicated places, and Tanner's teachers understood this. For some, the AYP determination was a signal that the school department's top leaders had misled them. "It's disappointing," said Fitzgerald, "because we've never had this label here at Tanner. I think a lot of the negativity that came with this administration affected our performance. And I might be the only one that feels that way, but when your teachers aren't happy, the kids aren't performing well. The science teacher put in for another job last year. I put in for another job. We lost our math teacher. And I won't say it was because of lack of support. I would say it was because of incompetence."

For Assistant Superintendent Ed Fellows, who had worked with Tanner for eleven years prior to the 2007 crisis, this view was in keeping his experience. "The teachers blame it on their principal not being an instructional leader. They would have the right to rationalize up the totem pole—that people somewhere at the top don't appreciate what they do. Or that it's not an effective place, and 'I'm not appreciated.'"

In her work with Tanner teachers as a math consultant, Mary Skinner saw a variation of this same thinking: the school's accountability status was both a reflection on its leadership and fundamentally its leaders' responsibility to address. "I don't think that the staff at Tanner has any sense of urgency," she said. "They did not get the message. I think that it's seen somehow as another initiative by the superintendent, even by the leadership—that it is not something that they are directly responsible for and that they could make the change to accomplish."

For other teachers, Tanner's AYP determination was rooted in some long-standing trends in the school district—trends with which they had disagreed for years. They pointed to how narrow the curriculum had become in the past several years and how few of the compelling programs that the school once offered now existed. After years of budget cuts and what they saw as an unrelenting pressure to teach more in less time,

teachers and students alike were burnt out and uninspired. Manopoulos, the hard-nosed attendance officer, was insistent about this. "It's all
about continued excessive instruction. Pound it into them. Let's go, let's
keep moving those kids. I don't think we offer kids that break." The
pressure extended to teachers and principals, too, he said. "You're a
principal. Do you really, after you've busted your ass to [get to school]
in the morning, say, okay, we have a meeting on curriculum now [at the
end of the day]? Don't you just want to digest what you've done for the
day and take a little break and maybe catch up on your notes, do your
e-mails? Maybe see the math teacher who did a great job that day based
on the lesson? Build some positives? Got to go right to work again, and
that stinks for kids, and it stinks for teachers."

To some, this new regime of testing, newspaper declarations, and
increased scrutiny felt like "MCAS indoctrination"; to others, the demands amounted to nothing less than a call to resist. "When you tell
somebody they have to do something," explained Lance Smith, a guidance counselor, "they don't want to do it. When you get them to want to
do it, it's a totally different thing. It's the same thing [with AYP]."

Fitzgerald saw an uncomfortable connection to her past in these new
requirements: "I went to Catholic school. They had this picture of a
communist leader hitting a kid over the head, and the kid's crying, to
show how evil the communists were because they were godless people.
For me, every time [the principal] starts with the MCAS, it's like, "Here
we go." It's MCAS-driven. It's not kid-friendly. It's not about kids; it's
about scores."

Over time, this reasoning goes, something has to give. In a system
in which teachers not only feel pressure, but are also being asked to
ignore their deep-rooted commitment to children, there is no positive
endgame. Smith concluded on a dour note: "I'm not pushing anyone so
far, but if there's [no sense that] we're all here to learn and it's kind of
a happy place to be, there's a backlash. At what point do you just keep
pushing people? At some point, they break, or there's a backlash."

For some, though, the school's AYP status occasioned no intense reaction at all. "I think that MCAS is this abstract notion to most teachers

in this school," explained another Hoover veteran. Then in her twenty-fifth year of teaching, Heather Tate felt she had a bead on her colleagues' view of accountability. "I think that teachers from K–4 don't really concern themselves with it that much. Grade four is the first year where it really counts. And I think grades seven and eight have consistently resisted it; they don't buy into it. They've been kind of waiting it out."

There was a question of legitimacy here; the MCAS couldn't go on forever, and its effect on individual teachers was less pointed than its effect on the school and its principal. Moreover, to some veteran teachers at least, the question of timing was important. "There's a strong parallel to why there's no [sense of urgency]," said Skinner. "You know, some teachers just say, 'I'll be going away. I'll be leaving, so MCAS isn't important. I just need to get by.' AYP is 2014."

These questions of causation and responsibility—who or what caused the school's recent "failure" and who ought to fix the problem—seemed to have broad implications for Tanner School, even in this early stage of its interaction with the state's accountability system. By December 2007, the school's principal had already started to formulate the school's response to this challenge, and she repeatedly encountered in her staff a reluctance to participate in discussions of strategies and an almost complete ennui about taking on additional responsibilities related to the MCAS.

Of course, it wasn't just teachers' feelings and views that counted in all this. Tanner came to its new accountability label having experienced a wide variety of initiatives and reforms over the previous several years, and these experiences also formed an important part of the school's story. During the previous three years, Tanner had felt like a busy place to work. Teachers were involved in an array of reform projects, from the now four-year-old effort to implement the challenging "Investigations" math program to more recent efforts to differentiate instruction, support the inclusion of special education students, and institute new positions related to teaching and learning. In a school like Tanner, where the school's publicized grade from the state accountability system was meant to spur new action and energize teachers, these efforts might have been called the foundation of the school's response to this system.

For a school with some history of collective expectations and organized change, its response to state accountability might have found fertile ground. But if the opposite were true—if a school had foundered either with its own initiatives or in its implementation of district expectations—then the preparation of a schoolwide response to accountability might have been significantly more complex. And just as the emotional responses of having been labeled "in need of improvement" had to include the voice of its teachers, Tanner's history of trying to improve instruction can be understood in the same manner.

For the past few years before 2007, the Tanner teachers had been asked to work on a practice called differentiated instruction, even if the teachers' definitions of this term had greatly wanted for consistency. Principal Waighn described the work toward differentiated instruction as one of the central tenets of her leadership. "The one thing I always say at professional development, at every meeting we have as a group, 'All kids can learn. They need more time, some of them. They need different strategies. But all kids can learn if we will give them the time.'" She then added, with a note of exasperation, "It's just that I'm not so sure that everybody believes it. They think, 'Oh, Johnny Smith's in resource room. He's dumb as a piece of mud. So he's never going to get this. I'm not spending the time with him.' Nobody has ever said that to me, but that's how I think it sometimes works. So I try to promote the thing that I'll come in and help them do: grouping. They never want me to do that."

Spotting an opportunity to build on summer coursework that a handful of Tanner teachers volunteered to take two years earlier, Waighn had these teachers make a series of presentations at her monthly faculty meetings. "I think [the training] was perceived well," said Tate. "I think people were open to it. But I think basically the people that [gave the monthly presentations] didn't have a goal in mind. Their teaching wasn't that great. They came in and said, 'We took this course, and it was really great, and here are the handouts from the course. Let's watch the video from the course.'" Other teachers felt similarly. "Last year's professional development was all about differentiated instruction," said

Smith. "But it wasn't on a concrete level, though. It was about ideas; it wasn't about 'try this and try that.' [If you have] three types of groups in your lesson, what would it take to make that happen? I think things got very simplified, but when you go to actually do it, and what you actually do—it wasn't clear."

Waighn was more positive, describing the impact of the presentations in terms of teachers' motivation, that is, their awareness that other types of instruction might be possible: "That was the one that woke them up about needing to do something about inclusion and differentiated instruction. Now, I see pieces of it happening. I think we have a long way to go with that, though. I think change is very, very slow in teaching. And if you expect leaps and bounds, you are going to be disappointed. If I can just see a little bit happen every month or every year even . . . "

The anecdotes about the inclusion of special education students in regular education classrooms had a similar feel: at a faculty meeting, the teachers were given information about inclusion and were then asked to make an earnest effort to adopt a new manner of working with these students. "It was a presentation," recalled Tate. "It was a lecture presentation. Take it or leave it. No follow-up. No nothing. And then this is the year that we are trying to really implement some inclusion models. I'm actually working one-on-one with one of the people that provided that training. And we just keep going around and around and around. Trisha gave us a handout from her initial training with some models for inclusion and what models do you think make sense." Tate's description jibed with Waighn's memory. "Well, we started with inclusion three years ago, and it was a hard thing because everybody's idea of inclusion was something different. And so, . . . I researched inclusion and came up with all these different models, and we discussed them at our team meetings. I let them pick which one they thought would work for them. It wasn't like, 'You're going to have it like this.'"

The result of both these multiyear efforts, one with differentiated instruction and one with inclusion, was that teachers continued to espouse a broad range of beliefs about both practices. Consequently, the consistent enactment of these changes was still far from complete. In my conversations with Tanner teachers about differentiation, there was ample difference in how teachers conceived of the idea. For some, differentiation represented a philosophy about grouping students for instruction; for others, it was about giving additional time for the completion of classroom assignments. For others still, it was about constructing and giving tests at a variety of levels. Teachers also defined differentiated instruction as the roles students might adopt during group work, as project-based learning, or as accepting a variety of learning styles as legitimate.

There was a similar struggle in the school to define a working model of inclusion, and nearly every teacher I spoke with described some level of conflict between regular education teachers and their special education counterparts on issues related to team teaching, lesson plans, student grouping, and grading. In an environment that the principal described as one that accommodates a range of preferences by teachers, it seemed that these preferences—all these preferences—were what prevailed. "What some teachers want is that the resource room will take over their classroom," Waighn said in reference to her teachers' thinking about inclusion. "And it isn't inclusion as I envision it. The resource room people are willing to do almost anything. And some classroom teachers are willing for me to do everything."

Tanner may well have had what one teacher called a pick-and-choose culture, where each teacher could determine, at his or her own discretion, what practices were employed in the classroom. Assistant Principal Bennett gave this impression of what she would see in her tours through the building: "[There's not much change in teaching] unless they change grade levels, I would say. I love our seventh-grade teacher; she's a wonderful language arts teacher, but she could be doing so much more. But she does her *Anne Frank* [unit] and her other things that she's been doing the same way. It's a wonderful presentation, and the kids really get involved in it, but there are so many other, more current things that she could be doing. Maybe if she did that, we could have a few more kids in the advanced [category of the MCAS]." In this formulation, her opinion of the language arts teacher's work was precisely that—a personal opinion—and it's not, in any case, meant as even constructive criticism. Bennett went on: "I personally think you should teach kids the way you would want your own children to be taught, or your own grandchildren. I think that you need to make accommodations, because in this particular school, we have some children from very low socioeconomic areas, the Projects and the Towers. [But teachers'] personality differences [interfere] a lot of the time. There is very little cross-grade integration." Though Bennett might have disagreed with what she saw happening in some classrooms, and though she was technically the supervisor to these teachers, she felt there was little she could do.

"Teachers have a lot of latitude in . . . their rooms," explained Addy Beckmann, a third grade teacher. This flexibility was lauded by some of the staff at Tanner; for others, it seemed to be the source of some frustration. One teacher, Celia Sonshak, described her experience at a recent faculty meeting when she proposed a common assessment in mathematics that she had seen during her tenure at another Hoover school. "I actually brought it up in a meeting. I didn't want to say, 'This is the way we did it over here.' I mean, everybody comes with ideas. You work in different buildings; you work for different administrations. You know, there are things that you pick and choose that you like, and there are things that you don't like. But I brought it to the table, and I know that the principal was really interested in that component. But now, what we are doing is kind of focusing on kids who need improvement through tutoring." Though Sonshak expressed no regret about her proposal, the idea did not fly with her colleagues and came to a quick end.

In fact, very few ideas in the school apparently stand as common expectations for instruction. Aside from some recent attention to implementing the small-reading-group component of a five-year-old English language arts (ELA) program, Principal Waighn described very few nonnegotiables in her school. "[Teachers] have a ninety-minute block in ELA and math. They keep telling me that's too long a block for little kids. So I'm asking them to take either twenty minutes to a half hour at the beginning of the ELA block, or twenty minutes to a half hour at the end of the math block, to try to look at areas that we need to improve on. I had run off all the MCAS tests since 2003. They are in my office. All [the teachers] have to do is take them and maybe do a writing assignment from one of the old tests or something like that in ELA. And hopefully, that is going to be the way things are done on the MCAS, if the teachers aren't already doing that. I have asked the teachers to do it, but I'm not sure it happens in all rooms."

It may be a stretch to consider this initiative a hard-and-fast expectation—the principal didn't, after all, copy the test questions for her teachers or work with them to construct writing prompts and rubrics. Nor did she ask the teachers to submit their students' work once the writing was completed. But it is, along with the five-year struggle to institute small-group-reading instruction, evidence of the tenacity of Tanner's pick-and-choose culture. Teachers work hard, they uniformly insisted, and they do it in the ways that suit their own preferences.

On this issue of expectations, Waighn was, after many years of negative supervisory experiences in Hoover, quite gun-shy. She was reluctant to insist on anything. The few times that she'd confronted a teacher on any issue, she came away burned by the interaction. At her last school, where she served as assistant principal, she said she went to the mat to reprimand an inferior teacher. After much personal pain, she gained nothing. "I think our hands are so tied with this contract from the teachers. To be honest with you, I can't tell you how many times I wrote up a second-grade teacher in another school. And absolutely nothing happened. A plan was put in place for her. She didn't follow the plan. And still nothing was done. So I feel, like, a sense of hopelessness to do something about [poor teaching]." More recently, Waighn took on an issue with two teachers who were taking their class out for daily, overextended periods of recess. "They go out to recess at eleven o'clock. So the special education teacher shows up for inclusion at the same time and the classes don't come in until a quarter to twelve. This is unacceptable. I've spoken to them once. I've spoken to them twice. What can I do to them? It got to the point that one of the teachers said to me, 'What are you [doing], spying on us?' I said, 'Yes. I want to make sure that the kids are learning. Yes, I am spying.'"

Despite the feeling that she possesses limited power with her staff, Waighn did make a point of visiting classrooms every day, if only to know what was going on in her school. The practice, however, appears to have cost her. "We believe in the sanctity of the time that we have with the children," complained Johnna Fitzgerald about the first year of Waighn's visits to her classrooms. "We're on, we're performing, we're teaching every single day, every single class, and interruptions are not welcome. And they're not welcome if it doesn't directly relate to us or the kids in front of us." Waighn recounted the same episodes from her rookie year as principal of Tanner: "Johnna said to me, 'You know something? When you used to come in, I hated it. I didn't like you being in there. I didn't like you invading my space.'" Three years later, Tanner teachers said they were more comfortable with the visits, which were clearly opportunities for administrators to engage socially with Tanner students; the visits were expressly not for viewing instruction and offering feedback. Assistant Principal Bennett, like Waighn, was clear about what she believed she could —and could not— do if she viewed in a classroom something that ran counter to own thinking. "If I go in and I'm not seeing things that are going so well, I'm not going to come right out and say that. I'll put that in a written form, an [annual] evaluation. This is an area of need, this is what you need to work on, this is what I need to work on. But I would never just say it." Bennett further explained that during her first year as assistant principal at Tanner, she was told she was contractually prohibited from taking notes during her daily visits to classrooms. The experience apparently warded off even verbal comments to teachers, and the likely result would be a system in which subpar practice was addressed only on an annual basis and progress was necessarily measured in years.

In light of what both Waighn and Bennett considered the unsolvable complications of setting clear expectations and confronting members of the faculty, each seemed to have invented her own way of inoffensively pressing for change. In effect, the two created frames for talking openly about the need to improve instruction and, though the frames were relatively unspecific, they were the motivational tools Waighn and Bennett relied on in the face of new pressures related to the school's AYP status. Lance Smith caught on, and he described Waighn's tactic fairly explicitly: "People are still just doing what they normally do . . . but now it is not good enough. So, what has to be different? Trisha's expression, what she says to teachers: 'We can't do the same old, same old.'" This was a comment echoed by many teachers at Tanner, and in interview after interview, they all seemed to understand their charge as one of innovation and change—even if they understood little about how their principal conceived of the quality of these changes. "So, you could do games and fun things," said Smith. "That's easy to say. But then tell me, what games do you want me to do? Do you want me to do a math club? Then tell me these are the five games that you do on this day and these are the ten games you do on this day. And I could do that. But, without that information, . . . it's mind-boggling."

Classroom teachers clearly had a similar understanding of the challenge represented by Tanner's new accountability status. They generally understood that classroom teaching at Tanner was already good, but that it might need something like a facelift. "Our lessons are already geared for success," Fitzgerald explained. "I know that in the upper grades, we work very hard on teaching MCAS skills throughout the year—so that we don't do an MCAS review the week before the test. They practice; they understand the questions. Our lessons are geared toward success on the test." Celia Sonshak, the teacher whom Waighn had unsuccessfully confronted about regularly shortening her math instruction in favor of an extended recess, had something similar to say about what the school needed to do: "We're classroom teachers. We're doing it. We think we're doing a very good job."

For Heather Tate, the imperative laid out by Waighn was more about calling the school's current set of practices by a new name than it was about renovating practices: "What kinds of things can we do to bring [the scores] up? The buzzword right now is differentiated instruction. But we have a lot of people that are doing that, differentiated teaching. You have a student that might be able to achieve all twenty-five problems on a paper. But you might have a person sitting next to them that only can do eight. We're trying to get them at a comfort level where they are certainly confident enough that they can get through those eight. And then, hopefully, we have the resource staff come in and help them, to even achieve the next set of questions or problems." There is nothing new about this notion of teaching—it accepts a lower level of performance from some students and relies on remedial support from special education when classroom instruction is insufficient—but with the right label, it becomes an example of one teacher's efforts to comply with Waighn's request to abandon the "same old, same old." Conceptually, there was a symmetry between Waighn's positions and those of many of her teachers.

There is a point to these stories about Tanner's experience with reform. They provide the background to the school's designation as an underperforming school, and while the school's experiences of change are not likely to fully determine its response to its new AYP status, the experiences will influence what school leaders believe is possible, what they attempt to do, and how they'll go about it. Inasmuch as the school had historically taken all its major reform cues from the district, it would be likely to continue to do so. Because of its continuing problems consistently implementing any particular teaching practice, the school's response to its new accountability status would probably affect only pockets of the school. Tanner's teachers came into the current school year divided, doubtful of one another's efforts, and resolute in their notion of teaching as a matter of individual preference. As a group, they shared no common thinking about what was behind their new designation as an underperforming school, and they were similarly divided about what to do about it. After enduring several years of resentment, Tanner's administrators now enjoyed at least a collegial relationship with their faculty, though there were clearly limits in what they could expect of their teachers. As a district, Hoover was in transition, and there was much confusion about the work that was important to the school. In the earliest stages of wrestling with the implications of being labeled an underperforming school, Tanner failed to take advantage of the perspective and learning from Hoover's other underperforming schools. As we will

see, it was in the throes of Tanner's own initial shock and disappoint-
ment that the school formulated its first efforts to address the concerns
of the state.

Tanner's Response to Its Underperforming Status

Several years before Tanner was declared an underperforming school,
the Massachusetts Department of Education (DOE) established requirements for schools with a significant history of underserving their students. Stoddard School, for example, which entered its fourth year of
corrective action in 2004, was compelled to complete PIM. Even during this period, though, the state had always conceived of the first several years of a school's "underperforming" designation as a period of
near-complete autonomy. In 2007, this level of autonomy continued,
and it was left to Tanner—along with Hoover officials—to develop the
school's plan.

In keeping with the general template of PIM and with the district's
own homegrown emphasis on the use of performance data, Tanner was
spending much of its organized meeting time on the most recent round
of MCAS results. For Principal Trisha Waighn, this task represented a
special challenge. For several weeks before she presented the data to her
staff at an afternoon faculty meeting, she had carted nearly one hundred pages of raw data from the school to her home, painstakingly poring over the school's results. Her notes from this work, handwritten on
page after page of yellow legal paper, became the source material for
these presentations, and aside from the small report on Tanner that she
downloaded from the DOE's Web site, these were the only handouts
available to her staff. She prepared grade-by-grade analyses of mathematics strands and ELA genres, comparisons of student strith in ' students
with multiple-choice questions, open-response questions, and longer essays; and studies of cohorts of students from one year to the next. She
isolated the questions with which the majority of students in a particular grade struggled most. She focused another analysis on each of the
school's student subgroups. Overall, she concluded, the scores were sim-

ply flat: where one group seemed to outscore its grade-level counterparts from the previous year, another group appeared in decline. In the aggregate, the school was making minimal progress, and its Composite Performance Index (CPI) scores—a cumulative index used by the DOE for the purpose of gauging a school's overall progress—just weren't good enough to satisfy the rising performance levels required under No Child Left Behind.

Among the teachers at Tanner, there was a telling confusion about what the data might require of them. The school's guidance counselor, Lance Smith, voiced this puzzlement: "So, in my mind, when you have a limited amount of resources, where do you take the resources and put them to the best use? I liken it to that little pop-up thing, [the Whack-a-Mole]. The head pops up, and you whack that one; this one comes up, you whack that one. Every year's [data] is different. There's no cohesive thinking about our turf . . . about creating a school culture."

Deb Perla, the school's curriculum team leader for mathematics, had a similar opinion of how the school had used its MCAS data so far: "[Teachers] know what we need, where we need to focus, but it's always different every year. I think we are frustrated as hell—I think we all are. We try to get a handle on [the data], and then it changes. We're all willing to do our piece, but I think MCAS has taken over our ability to be spontaneous within the class. Our school day is so structured now, especially with having to teach science and social studies every day. I think there is less wiggle room." For Perla, there was a special challenge in knowing how to focus on data that were available only once a year and that arrive nearly half a year after children were assessed. Johnna Fitzgerald was even more skeptical; she wasn't sure how anyone could form an accurate conclusion about a single grade level—or about a single teacher—when each year's test measured the progress of an entirely different group of students.

Instead of a conversation about particular teaching strategies, Waighn preferred to emphasize the importance of teachers' thinking about their classes as a few groups of differently performing students: "What we need to do is [think] about how can we move a group of these kids up, whether they be the 'warnings,' whether they be the 'needs improve-ments,' whether they be 'proficients.'" The notion was the backbone of her plan for achieving AYP that year. She directed her guidance coun-selor to target students for a special after-school remediation program, and she urged her teachers to think about how to advance each group of students in their classes. Somehow, however, the translation of this message—that the school should develop for each group of students its own opportunities for learning and its own teaching strategies—came to lack this universal, all-students-can-learn quality.

"We'll have two groups a week," said Celia Sonshak, the school's de-partment chair for social studies and a volunteer in a new after-school tutoring effort. "But this is a different approach. It is not reinventing the wheel, but [this year] we're focusing on the 'needs improvement' group rather than the 'warning' group. We really want to target 'needs improvement,' to see if we can bring them up." The strategy, at least as it was understood by Sonshak and other department chairs, was to de-vote more of the school's resources—teachers' in-class attention and op-portunities for after-school help—to students on the cusp of achieving a "proficient" score on the MCAS. "It's just statistics in the school," she explained. "I don't think we did as well as we've done in other years, so we're trying to step up to the plate and just try different things." The school would have had a better chance of achieving its AYP target if it had focused on students whose statistical "worth" was the greatest; a student who moves from the "warning" category to "needs improve-ment" is worth fewer points toward the school's CPI score than a stu-dent who moves from "needs improvement" to "proficient."

Addy Beckmann spoke about the problem of the students in the mid-dle. "[It started with a] conversation saying, 'I'm open for ideas. What do you think we should do? In the past, I've thought about it as needing to help the kids at the very bottom—maybe my focus should be those kids. Now, maybe my focus should be the middle class, you know, aver-age kids that always seem to get skipped over. If you're way up high and you are doing really well, you get attention, or if you're way at the bot-tom, you get very much attention. The kids in the middle always seem to get lost. So I'm going to shift it. I'm going to try something different because I want to try helping the average student go one level above and maybe get into the 'proficient' level." Beckmann saw several implications of this shift in her focus: "I used to focus all my tutors coming in from the local university on the ones who were really down in the dregs and failing. This year, . . . they're helping the average kid, the students who are in need of improvement, not [those at the 'warning' level]. I can't predict it's going to help . . . But, you know, sometimes you can only offer so much help. Sometimes those kids are just going to be in that area. If they do improve, it's within that same realm." In a world of limited time and resources, went Beckmann's estimate, it's most prudent to invest where you're likely to get the return.

In my conversations with Tanner administrators and teachers, it became clear that the new after-school tutoring—with its focus on middle-performing students—was the centerpiece of the school's efforts to achieve AYP that year. Described first to Hoover principals by the superintendent at the close of October and expected to be up and running by the start of December, the tutoring program was meant to be the main programmatic remedy to the district's flagging test scores. Superintendent Steve Halstrom asked his principals to recruit teachers for up to four additional hours per week and to aggressively seek out the students most likely not to be served by any of the district's other after-school programs. As was the district's custom, the tutoring program was to pay teachers at their contractual hourly rate, twenty-two dollars an hour, for instructional time only; teachers were expected to plan lessons for the program on their own time. If materials were necessary, the schools were asked to pick up these costs from their own budget.

For Principal Waighn, though, the tutoring program came with a bevy of headaches and was a fair degree shy of a thoughtful response to the school's challenges. As she tried to explain at a meeting of principals, all the Tanner faculty members who were interested in paid after-school opportunities were already engaged as teachers in the school's 21st Century Learning Center program, a large, federally funded after-school program that had operated in the district for three years and to which after-school teachers had already made a semester-long commitment in September. In the same way, many of the students to be targeted by the school for intervention were already members of the 21st Century program, and their parents had proved reluctant to forgo the program's enrichment clubs in favor of test preparation and remediation. Waighn was likewise frustrated by the long-delayed arrival of test-preparation materials she had requisitioned months earlier, and she was throwing in the towel on her well-established Saturday program at Tanner because of a recent concession to the school custodians union. (The agreement required the presence of a custodian for any extracurricular event and would have given fully a third of her small Saturday program's funds to a single custodian.)

More than anything, though, Waighn's effort to launch the superintendent's tutoring program at Tanner was beleaguered by a reluctance among Tanner teachers to join the effort. In the view of some teachers, their distance from the tutoring program was something of a boycott. Lance Smith counted himself as one of Waighn's key supporters in the school, but he believed he represented many teachers in their objection to another "top-down" imposition on their school: "[Teachers] are working really hard, and the feeling is you're not good enough, whatever you did. And now they're going to want you to do after-school programs for another [few hours a day]. It's another command—it's a demand on people—and people are feeling stressed as it is." Yvette Bennett concurred, but noted that Tanner had always struggled to recruit members of the staff for responsibilities beyond the teaching day: "There's always been an ongoing problem here. People see their day as done at 2:30, and they're ready to go home. Unfortunately, that's not the way the school system will be going in a few years."

By December, Waighn was able to launch the superintendent's tutoring program at Tanner, but she did so having been forced to recruit teachers from other Hoover schools; the voluntarism among her own staff was just too sparse to accommodate even a modest number of students. The teachers' feelings about the tutoring program—strained feelings of autonomy that so characterized the Tanner staff—evidently applied to this effort as well. In fact, responsibility for the school's performance on the MCAS for the upcoming year seemed to lie entirely with the principal. The teachers referred to the program as "Trisha's deal" or as something to be optimistic about, even if there was only limited commitment to its success. "Trisha is going to be running this Tuesday and Thursday MCAS camp, which is going to be good," said Sonshak. "[In the past] MCAS camps have been running four-day programs on vacation. So this might be a little different angle that she's got. So it will be interesting to see if it made a difference."

There were other efforts at Tanner related to the school's accountability status. Much in the vein of the superintendent's MCAS tutoring, the school had also been asked to open an academic drop-in center late in the previous school year. This request was part of the plan the district was required to submit to the DOE as a consequence of its own underperforming status. The centers were based on a design that Halstrom had heard about in a neighboring city. In essence, they amounted to a small sum of money to pay part-time aides to keep each school's library open until 6:00 p.m. Waighn's troubles with this initiative sounded much like her frustrations with the MCAS tutoring directive: there was little time for implementation, and she had no qualified volunteers from Tanner. What's more, she couldn't reconcile the school's after-hours security needs with the necessity of keeping at least one exterior door of the school open—well after dark—to comply with the requirement that students be permitted to visit the center on a drop-in basis. Waighn either had to organize an effort in the fashion of another after-school program—with schedules, parent permission forms, snacks, and outside supervision—which would mean her staying each night until 6:00 to serve as the program's administrator, or could let the effort slide. In the end, Tanner's drop-in center was an idea that just didn't fit.

Johnna Fitzgerald scoffed when I asked her about the center. "It's nothing," she remarked. "I think they're hoping for after-school programs to remediate a lot of the problems." Mary Skinner, the math consultant, was part of the district-level planning that resulted in the notion of drop-in centers in each school. She saw a general impatience on the part of the district if there was any mention of the challenges in bringing them to life. "The district was in corrective action, and I think that [this] was a pressure that drew us into the tight corner, and we fed into it. We started trying to address it as a quick fix instead of sitting back and doing a needs assessment. This [should have been] a three- to five-year plan. We're not going to come out of being in that hole overnight, and I think that's what they tried to do. Having the after-school program Centers of Excellence was just a title."

By December 2007, only a few months after Tanner had learned it was an underperforming school, the school's efforts to meet AYP in its March and May testing sessions had an uncertain, provisional quality. Waighn's request that her teachers take time from their daily English and math instruction to provide students the experience of responding to writing prompts based on the MCAS had taken hold in only a few classrooms. The efforts to broaden the base of teachers who regularly differentiated their teaching appeared to be stalled, and Waighn saw that the next stage of this project would bring her into unwanted conflict with teachers who held fast to their own styles of instruction. A few weeks earlier, in late November, the requisition for test-preparation materials—a request that Waighn had prepared over the summer—had still not been converted into a purchase order by the city's finance department. She had made a start with the superintendent's tutoring program, but with only a handful of her own staff, and out of necessity she planned to merge the program entirely with the school's 21st Century after-school program when the second semester began in January. The academic drop-in center was an on-paper-only endeavor. Her staff was still shocked by the AYP determination and more than a little angry. And at least some teachers had come away from recent faculty meetings about the MCAS thinking that the new imperative involved an increased attention to the needs of middle-performing students—not the low-performing students, who, it was reasoned, were probably already enrolled in special education. Throughout the school, teachers believed deeply that they were a hardworking and dedicated group and that they could do little more to improve achievement without great and unacceptable personal expense.

What Went Wrong at Tanner School: Four Common Intervention Mistakes

In some ways, all these issues are something akin to static on the airwaves. Understandably, the school would pass through a period of transition as it received news that it was an underperforming school and as—over a period still undetermined at Tanner—this news dislodged for staff and parents the notion that the school was good enough. All schools have their strengths and weaknesses related to implementation; all schools launch new efforts amid the detritus of past reforms; all schools have their politics. There was nothing novel in any of these observations at Tanner. These small problems exist in countless variations in every school, and the school leaders' job is to help bridge the gap between the daily shortcomings in money, material, motivation, and talent with their own vision of what is possible. Responding to small problems is what school administrators do. Worth more exploration at Tanner are the fixed problems—the beliefs and assumptions that appeared to define how school improvement was approached and that, much more fundamentally, set the stage for the work to come. The school and the district evinced larger patterns of thought and behavior in defining problems, bringing resources to these problems, and deciding what was possible. The following pages summarize the four major patterns that hindered Tanner's ability to engage in effective intervention.

School District's Inability to Recognize Patterns of Failure

Consider my conversation with Steve Halstrom, Hoover's superintendent, when he asserted that Tanner School was past agonizing about not having made AYP. Halstrom described an initial citywide reaction and the subsequent learning process after the DOE's publication of the list of the state's underperforming schools. "I think the people who got tagged early and are now in corrective action . . . led the charge of the shock of everything . . . and everyone has learned from that." He explained that the other Hoover schools, all of which were ultimately tagged as underperforming, had learned from these early-underachieving schools. The scramble, he believed, was over. People had wiped away the tears and dealt with their anger, and they were now ready to get to work.

Halstrom's assertions notwithstanding, there appeared to be nothing at all like a rub-off effect in the Hoover school district. As Hoover added new schools to its list of underperfoming institutions, it did so without any evident institutional accumulation of knowledge or any emotional buffer. Tanner School seemed bound to go through the same threat to its identity that had happened years earlier to other schools in Halstrom's district. And because of administrative turnover, weak relationships between school principals and central office leaders, or inadequate attention to the issues surrounding the "underperforming" designation, none of the district's accumulated knowledge helped Tanner's efforts to implement new strategies.

With this perception gap in play, the Hoover district asked Tanner School to implement an identical version of the strategies required of Jefferson, a school in its fifth year of corrective action. Indeed, on this question of capacity, there was no apparent acknowledgment that Tanner might have limited capacities for engaging in key aspects of data-based, standards-driven reform at this early stage of its improvement trajectory. Its capacity to use performance data had thus far been limited to the principal's handwritten notes, which were only delivered orally to the staff and were apparently understood in many different ways by teachers.

Tanner's school improvement plans were still prescribed by the district and would continue to be highly politicized and circumscribed affairs as long as principals were required to make annual public presentations of their plans, on television, to the Hoover School Committee. The school had a spotty track record with classroom-based improvement, and its pervasive culture of individualism and connoisseurship remained intact in the face of its new accountability status. The scrambling—for an understanding of what it meant to be in need of improvement, for a foothold with strategies for helping all students achieve at higher levels, or simply to comply with the state requirements associated with this group of schools—that the superintendent insisted had ended throughout Hoover's schools seemed not even to have begun at Tanner. In fact, neither the district nor the DOE had even rattled Tanner's cage.

Inadequate Attention to the Instructional Core

For Tanner, there might have been a real and lasting significance to this early stage of existence as an underperforming school. Clearly, it was a time when the principal and staff would have had to reconceptualize their school, and a relatively nuanced and receptive strategy for helping the staff understand themselves both as competent, committed, and needing to work in new ways would have been required. Nothing from my conversations with Tanner faculty indicated quite how long this process would have taken, even if it had been well supported, but at least some part of the first year, if not all of it, would have been needed to attend to this issue.

Waighn was paying attention to this need, even if Halstrom was convinced that it was not there, but she did so in ways that might have proved problematic if the year's efforts yielded no fruit. She was publicly resolute in her statements that Tanner's teachers already knew everything they needed to know to meet the challenge of AYP; she framed the imperative for instructional improvement exclusively in terms of resisting the tug toward the "same old, same old"; and she largely accepted the responsibility placed on her by both the staff and the central office to address student achievement problems through extracurricular remediation.

Pushed out a few years, the plan would hardly seem a robust model for sustained improvement. Teachers may never feel that there are compelling expectations related to changes in their teaching practice; they may never view their work in terms of the results they produce for every child they serve; and they might continue to work in isolation, possibly with an even greater cynicism about their leaders' inability to fix the school's problems. Getting this first stage of state accountability right may not be so much about recruiting students for after-school tutoring or settling on a single strand of the mathematics frameworks to emphasize at a particular grade level. These problem-specific strategies do little to lay a base for ongoing future improvements in classroom teaching. It's much more about establishing the conditions for productive and ongoing improvement to the school's core—the critical processes of instruction and assessment—taken on in an open way with teachers, with expert support, and in the context of increasing, mutually reinforced expectations. There was strikingly little evidence that this foundation was being laid at Tanner. In fact, much evidence suggested that throughout the Hoover school district, this essential question about the quality of the instructional core was being given short shrift.

To better understand this point about improving core work, ask yourself some questions about Tanner's efforts thus far. Did Tanner and its district hold that classroom teaching was the most significant determinant of student success in its control? Did the school place strategies to improve the quality of classroom teaching at the center of its improvement effort? Did it espouse some theory about how to improve classroom instruction, and did it build—or was it building—a structure of professional development and support that would reasonably produce these changes over a few years? Did the school and district leaders discuss how they were going about this kind of work?

Considering the school's programmatic response to its AYP designation and its efforts over the last several years, the improvement of classroom teaching did not seem to be Tanner's primary goal. In both the school and the district, there existed an overall sense that the core of classroom teaching was fundamentally good enough. Among all the respondents in Hoover—from the superintendent and other central office leaders to the principal and her teachers—the most widely referenced effort related to the school's AYP status was the superintendent's tutoring program. Clearly, there were daunting administrative challenges related to launching this program: the tight timeline of only six weeks; the conflict in timing, student enrollment, and staffing with the school's already-existing 21st Century program; the budget shortfalls; teachers' near-universal concerns about low pay and the absence of compensation for preparation time; and the hold-up on test tutoring materials purchased three months earlier. These things, while they might have been approached more thoughtfully, are common challenges for most administrators, and Waighn didn't let them stop her.

More worrisome about the tutoring program, however, especially when it is viewed from the perspective of efforts to improve the school's instructional core, was the lack of a complementary and systematic plan to plug the gaps in the quality of Tanner's classroom teaching. The professional development rested entirely on the willingness of some staff members to make presentations to their colleagues about training they had attended. The school had no day-to-day capacity either for establishing expectations that teachers would try new strategies or for supporting teachers' learning if the strategies proved to be difficult. The coaching in mathematics was haphazard; after five years in the school, Skinner was still unable to work with teachers in their classrooms or to observe teachers doing their work, and teachers who wished to opt out of any interaction with her were perfectly able to do so. There was no complementary coaching resource in any other subject area. No one in the school, short of the principal, had any coherent idea of what teaching practices were expected of every teacher at Tanner, and even the principal, burned many times by tiring conflicts with the teachers union, felt her best option for supporting her expectations was simply to hope that they came to pass.

Misinterpreting Knowledge for Willingness to Change

One part of this separation between school-day and after-school improvements may have resided in another aspect of the relationship between Hoover's central office and its principals. At this level in Hoover's administrative chain, there was a form of quid pro quo thinking in which central office administrators appeared to trade material and political support in clear exchange for what they assumed to be principals' expertise on matters of instructional leadership. Where it concerned the implementation of new teaching strategies in every classroom in the city, the district's entire administrative operation seemed to extend no further than the office of the principal.

Superintendent Halstrom described how the trade worked: "If you come to work here—this is your job. Professional development started to take on an air of conversation, at least that was the goal: Give principals time to meet with staff, and support [them with] money and substitutes and food, whatever they needed to create an environment where teachers and principals could work through their issues. And when data started to come back to us at the local level, [we asked] 'How do you want to handle this data at the local level?'" In the same way, principals in Hoover were more hamstrung by their reluctance to agitate for change than they were by any limitation in their own knowledge of teaching and professional development. "Bluntly," Halstrom continued, "principals [must recognize] that they need to be more accountable about walking into a room and doing some informal observations of student learning and seeing that good teaching and good curriculum was being managed in as much of the school as possible—by designating those areas that needed improvement and coming up with an action plan." In this view, if anything was missing in Hoover and at Tanner, it was courage, not knowledge—and the central office, inasmuch as it had delivered to the schools what it had promised, was right to expect that principals take the ball to the hoop and lay it in.

It was precisely the district's faith in its principals' knowledge of teaching and change that led to its distance in these areas. For her part, Waighn adopted a similar stance to instructional leadership in her work with Mary Skinner. When Skinner came to Tanner each month, Waighn provided little direction or planning for her and often left unspecified even the names of the teachers Skinner should work with. The content of the coaching workshops was Skinner's to plan, and she often had only a single point of contact with a particular teacher in a given school year. "If I wasn't coming back for three more months," lamented Skinner, "it's kind of a waste of time. You still get something done, but I don't feel that there's that closure. . . . [T]here is no follow-up." Waighn felt similarly about her work with the central office administrators: "They left me to fly on my own."

All of this is an arrangement that misses what is important: it continually disregards the need to build the skills of Hoover's administrators and teachers. It assumes that people know something they don't. Central office administrators either trusted that principals knew how to improve the teaching of every member of their staff or believed that principals just needed to start doing their jobs. Principals expressly trusted the capacity of the district's single coach to affect teaching. And teachers trusted that principals could fix their school's shortcomings by managing initiatives that required none of their time and effort. In all this trusting, there was great discontent and a great disregard for the question of capacity and knowledge. If the principal and teachers already knew what to do to serve the school's neediest children, then an entire line of action—an entire vein of leadership—was simply superfluous to the task. If principals and teachers really didn't know what to do, and no one was thinking seriously about what this meant, then Tanner's new AYP status was unlikely to produce anything other than simple pressure on the people in the organization. And pressure alone is probably a sorely inadequate leavening for any school.

Substituting the District's Needs for the School's

In another important respect—the obligations of the Hoover school district to the state—Tanner School was very different from Stoddard. In 2004, when Stoddard School was in the throes of its fourth year of corrective action, there were only a very limited number of requirements placed on the Harborview Public Schools with respect to No Child Left Behind. The district itself had no accountability status, and the state DOE interacted directly with Stoddard School about performance improvement mapping, largely without contact with the district. Harborview, as an integral party to the improvement of Stoddard, was, in practical terms, not even invited to the table. By 2007, though, when Tanner School was first declared to be in need of improvement, the state had taken action to solve the steadily mounting challenge of dealing with so many individual schools, and this particular aspect of state intervention policy had changed very dramatically. The state had abandoned the PIM plan, had ceased its school inspections, had created a system for grading school districts, and was focused nearly exclusively on its relationships with central office administrators and superintendents as the primary form of its intervention and support. So, when Tanner moved into the "in need of improvement" category for the first time, Hoover Public Schools, as a collective, had already been declared to be in corrective action, and the district was required to submit its own action plan to the state. Though the new state policy provided no guidance on the primacy of either the district's or the school's accountability status, these two designations now coexisted, and Tanner very clearly needed to comply with Hoover's improvement plan.

On the ground, then, Tanner School had already begun to respond to the mandatory plan to remedy the district's accountability status before it was ever labeled by the state. The academic drop-in center initiative from the previous school year and the superintendent's after-school remediation program represented two key requirements of this plan. The district expected that every Hoover school would initiate these programs, irrespective of a particular school's accountability designation. The department chair positions were also borne of the district's attempt to provide coaching to all schools in corrective action, as were a set of formative assessments that the district had designed and recently instituted.

From the perspective of these two schools—Stoddard and its obligations to the state, and Tanner with its district-imposed requirements—it was a question of whether one master had been replaced with another. At Stoddard, the teachers' sense of obligation to comply with the tenets of PIM was intense and pervasive. This obligation was the single rationale that every member of the school's PIM team could invoke when speaking to a colleague about why change was necessary. Compliance became something like a mantra, and this obligation, not student achievement, became the new goal for everyone in Stoddard. At Tanner, the pressure to comply was equally obvious, but was unaccompanied by any sense of ownership. For Waighn, the drop-in centers and the superintendent's tutoring program were not her ideas. They didn't make sense to her, mainly because they duplicated what the school was already doing and because the number of teachers who would work after school had already peaked. When she complied, she didn't feel that she was at least working on her own agenda; she had the begrudging air of someone doing another person's work. And this sense of an external burden leaked into the thinking of her staff: as much as Waighn placed ownership and responsibility for the success of these programs with her boss, Tanner's teachers placed ownership for the same programs with Waighn.

This all may be too fine a distinction to make, except that so much has been written about just how important a school's sense of its own responsibility and efficacy really is. Clearly, the compliance attitude was a problem at both schools, and from the view afforded through a school's front door, it may be of only marginal importance whether demands are coming from the state or the district. Either way, it seems, teachers felt cynical and fatalistic, and administrators felt disempowered. What is different, however, is that Stoddard was required to comply with a process designed to increase its own independence and problem-solving capabilities, even if this work had produced little of either after two years. Tanner, in contrast, had to direct its limited energies to manning programs that were not of its own design. And especially problematic is that when Tanner made these efforts, the school might have had less incentive to examine its own internal workings. When it created after-school programs and satisfied the dictates of the district's improvement plan, the school had done its job and made what it considered satisfactory effort to address the state's concerns. These steps also lessened the school's need to look inside its own classrooms and create its own more meaningful plan for improving classroom teaching. The difference in outcomes may be negligible; the difference in intent is enormous.

3

Connington School: Seven Years in Intervention

I n the opening weeks of September 2007, Connington School was an engaged place. Now entering its eighth year of restructuring as a chronically underperforming school, the current year was clearly imbued with a sense of weight and urgency, and for the principal, Jesse Martinez, it had the quality of a last stand. After so many challenges over the last five years of his tenure, this was the year to get it right. This was the year for all the planning, the clashes with veteran teachers, the painstaking hiring of an almost entirely fresh staff, and the wrestling with the city's cumbersome school bureaucracy to yield something positive for Connington's students. It was a make-or-break year for the elementary school ranked as one of the state's worst.

To the outside observer, the plans at Connington to pull up its test scores were ambitious. The majority of the school's students were organized into no less than three instructional groups, and its specialist staff—bolstered with many community volunteers—attempted to intervene with struggling students in three successive tiers, the last of which provided intensive, nearly one-to-one tutoring for the students who most needed it. The school's instructional coaches were working in every classroom to support the teachers as they implemented the school's curricula. The teachers, in turn, were organized into an impressive array of professional groups: The school had separate leadership teams for reading, writing, math, and English language learners; teachers met weekly with their grade-level counterparts with agendas that were established by the principal and each of the four leadership teams; and for the first time that year, members of each leadership team were conducting their own "learning walks," observing the classrooms of their peers to understand patterns in the implementation of the school's teaching goals and to target professional development. The whole school, from kindergarten to fifth grade, had established a special instructional period—what teachers loosely called AYP time (for adequate yearly progress)—to prepare students to take the Massachusetts Comprehensive Assessment System (MCAS) exams. Teachers were required each month to submit the results of a host of assessment data in reading, writing, and math, and each team regularly dedicated time to study these formative data. There were protocols for what classrooms should look like and for what teachers should be doing with students as their workday proceeded, and the curricula in each subject area were well organized and methodically paced. As the new school year opened, Connington was ready to enact each part of its elaborate plan, and there was little reason to believe—at least until the previous year's MCAS scores came in at the beginning of October—that the effort wouldn't yield the results the school longed for.

As the third school in this book, Connington share only some of the features that define Stoddard and Tanner. Like the teachers at the other two schools, Connington teachers continued to sort out—sometimes with a sense of great confusion and pain, and even after eight years in restructuring—the meaning of their school's worrisome test scores. Connington, however, had weathered the storm of its first years as an underperforming school, and its reactions were markedly different, if no less poignant. The school faced dramatically different circumstances. It had no direct involvement with the state, but the city school district was decidedly more active in its stance on student learning and professional development. As a result, Connington was greatly influenced by these district initiatives, both in its structure and its approach.

Connington also has its own narrative, one that is distinct from the two schools that precede it. At the Stoddard School, the performance improvement mapping (PIM) intervention placed teacher-leaders in the position of having to comply with the formal requirements of PIM while also managing the pressing tensions of staff politics and school culture. Their decision making in this second realm had profound implications for PIM and for their school. At Tanner, professionals in every level of the school system—from the teachers to the principal to the superintendent—appeared to view the challenges of state accountability as primarily an exercise in compliance, and this view did little to counteract the school's historically very removed treatment of classroom teaching and teacher learning. Quite in contrast, the larger narrative at Connington School settled on the profound tension between tight central control—in this case, by the school's principal—and the teachers' homegrown accountability. At Connington, data were taken seriously, classrooms were not private realms, and expectations for instruction were explicit and strongly enforced. But these features were the hard-won result of the principal's direct control and weren't necessarily compatible with the teachers' sense of efficacy, creativity, and professional growth. They didn't yet make for a school where students achieved. Though Connington exhibited many of the popular hallmarks of reform—the nearly uniform implementation of several promising programs, coaching for teachers, systems for data analysis, and structures for professional communication—its scores were actually in decline. This chapter will look at what caused this apparent paradox.

Reactions to the Connington's Accountability Status

One peculiarity of large-scale testing in Massachusetts is that the schools must wait six months for the results of the previous year's exams. Consequently, the professional staff of Connington, with the school year already under way, felt thoroughly blasted when they finally learned that the school's results were worse than any year since the inception of the MCAS in 1999. The school's scores in English language arts, long a thorny subject and the principal cause of the school's designation as chronically underperforming, took a sharp dive; in mathematics, where the school had met its AYP goals in the past, the scores showed a similar, precipitous drop. Connington would spend another year as one of the few dozen Massachusetts schools in restructuring status, and for everyone at the school, the news was a disaster.

"I had no idea," said Aaron Carpenter, a young second-year teacher at Connington. "Just to see that the school I'm working at right now, to see that we're 984th [in the state]—at least the fourth-graders were 984th in reading, 979th in math. I was absolutely shocked. I was honestly blown away."

"I think still we're in the shock-and-awe phase of getting the data back," said Jimmie Stanzer, with much the same impression as his colleague. "It was low. You know, I'm invested in the fourth grade, and I'm invested in the school. I know the good things that go on here, and I know the bad, too, but to me, it's like, wow, there are about 670 better fourth grades in the state than us." To both teachers, what was most striking about the results, and most damning, was that hardly any other school in the state produced less promising results. And what was worse, both educators knew very well that the school was struggling. But they had thought that the hard work, the cutting-edge strategies, and the years of reinventing the staff were supposed to have brought something other than continued failure.

To some teachers at Connington, something about their colleagues' reaction to the discouraging news was reminiscent of how the same discouraging news broke in the earliest years of the school's troubles with the MCAS. Jessica Hereford, a fourth-grade teacher, recalled that in the first few years of the state's accountability system, when Connington was first designated as an underperforming school, teachers were quick to look at the shortcomings of their students' upbringing. At that point in the school's development, teachers had little inclination to consider the MCAS results a product of the school's own efforts. In her view, this thinking about the cause of students' failure on the MCAS changed very gradually, mainly because increasing numbers of the staff began to accept the school's plans to get better. "I'd say [the blaming] became less strong as people started focusing on these different interventions. But it's still there when we have these conversations—especially with our latest MCAS results, which were not strong. The school has been going through all these changes—all this work. Well, we're really . . . implementing all these interventions—so why isn't it working?"

All across the school, the mood was somber and more than a little doubtful of the year's work. If we were engaged in a full-court press last year and we still lost the game, they reasoned, does it still make sense to use the same strategy to play the next one? Didn't everyone say that these strategies, if we really did them, would work? Martinez feared that this feeling would infect his young staff. For him, the real concern lay in his knowing that he finally had the team he wanted at Connington. He saw real progress in the adoption of teaching techniques that were more promising, and for the first time, he was generally impressed by the level of professionalism, focus, and determination he saw in his teachers. He now needed wind in the sails, not such deflating, dampening news. "My teachers can be angry about the scores. They can be demoralized about them and still build their resolve around it. What I don't want people saying is, 'See, all of this additional effort being strategic, it isn't paying off.' And certainly, I don't want people saying, 'See, this population is never going to produce.'"

Connington's student population was a diverse group with numerous challenges. With 540 students of mostly Puerto Rican, Dominican, and African American heritage, the school was one of the city of Huntington's larger elementary schools and one of the district's most programmatically varied buildings. Serving students from kindergarten through fifth grade, the school hosted various specialized programs for students from throughout the same geographical zone. Children with limited proficiency in English could be assigned to the school's sheltered English instruction (SEI) program, and there were four "lab" classrooms—intensive special education settings for students with severe behavioral and emotional challenges. Of the four classrooms at nearly every grade level at Connington, one was devoted to SEI instruction and another to special education, and the size of these two programs was growing each year. Over the preceding three years, the district administration had added the SEI program to Connington and had added a lab class each year as well. Almost every student at the school qualified for a free or reduced-price lunch—a common school indicator of poverty—and one of three students was new each year, having transferred from another city school, from another city, or, quite frequently, from another country. The expanding mix of programs and similarly shifting student population were not lost on anyone at Connington. But, Martinez said, these shifts had not in recent years dominated the teachers' thinking in an unproductive way.

Like every complex organization, there was a story on Connington's surface and another one somewhere below. On the surface, Connington had endured many years of difficult changes—most notably in the composition of its staff, its instructional programming, and its orientation toward classroom teaching as the key determinant in the success of its students. Open resistance to change was no longer an issue; the vast majority of teachers were open to new ideas. Below the surface, however, was a more nuanced view of the school. Connington was nowhere near a finished product and, understandably, was not in a position to dramatically improve its outcomes. In fact, it may have only been starting a second, even more daunting stage of a school looking to improve. In some crucial ways, the school was still haunted by the turmoil of its earliest years of wrestling with state accountability. To understand where things went wrong, we need to look back to when the school first learned of its underperforming school designation—a moment that coincided with Martinez's arrival as the principal of Connington School.

Reactions to State Accountability

"Connington is a complex place, and I'm just beginning to understand its characteristics," explained Jessica Hereford. "It's interesting, because I came to Connington in Jesse's second year. And at that point, the school was already in restructuring. It seems like when he first got here, there were a lot of teachers who were very resistant to change, very resistant to kind of mixing things up. When I got here, we were just starting to be a Reading First school, and there was all this kind of pressure as far as the DOE [Massachusetts Department of Education] was involved." (Reading First is a federal grant program pursued by Martinez in his early years as principal.) Hereford went on to describe the resistance she saw among her colleagues, mainly in terms of ownership and responsibility. It seemed to her that teachers' concerns were then primarily centered both on the validity of the state exam as a measure of the work they did with poor, urban children and on a kind of simmering resentment toward the new principal's abrupt, controlling style. "The dynamic has changed," she said. "There are a lot more things like teacher leadership; there's a lot more ownership growing right now than what we had before. To me, . . . one of the major characteristics of Connington is that it is in flux; it's in development in certain ways. But it's been a rocky road to get there."

With eight years at Connington, Jimmie Stanzer was one of the school's most senior teachers. "Coming here," he said, "I didn't know what I was getting into. I came from a psychiatric unit working in a children's hospital, and . . . it was a big change. People had never really been held accountable, I don't think. The whole No Child Left Behind . . . Now we've got to make schools accountable, classrooms accountable, kids accountable—and I think that increased the negativity, because now people were asking, 'Why are these kids not passing, and what are we going to do to get them up to speed?' Those . . . questions really caused a lot of anxiety among staff, because we did have a little bit of an older staff. Some people were here twenty, twenty-five years, and they probably were never . . . confronted about what really was going on. It was, okay, you had thirty kids, you do your report cards, you send your report cards home, you keep them in the classroom—and everyone thinks you're learning."

Stanzer, too, noted that for many teachers, Martinez became the symbol of this new accountability and that his demands, whether transmitted through him from the state or of his own design, smacked of a heretofore unknown tyranny. "If I was [teaching] something for so long and there was no measurement stick that said what was working, and all of a sudden, bang, we're looking at these data . . . Forty percent of these kids are failing, and eighteen of them are in your class, so what's going on in your class? I think people took that personally. It reflected, I think unintentionally, on the administrators because they're usually the ones that have the data to tell us—they're the ones usually facilitating the meetings. And I think people believed that this guy is a jerk and we don't like him."

At the time, another aspect of the reaction to the school's new accountability status was much like the reaction of the current Connington staff and Tanner's and Stoddard's staffs when these educators heard about their schools' underperformance: people felt exasperation, disbelief, and defeat; they felt that their efforts were impugned. "What else can we do?" asked Hereford, remembering the period. "A lot of teachers were very overwhelmed; [there was] a lot of fear. What does restructuring mean? They were a little overwhelmed with the task of looking at their whole school improvement plan and making improvements, because I think at that time, people felt like they were working hard and they didn't know why it wasn't working."

By all accounts, the period that followed this shock, disbelief, and anger toward the new principal was one of open conflict, mass resignations, and an unprecedented tightening of control. This phase of the school's existence lasted several years, and in the view of many, including Martinez, it was only now beginning to conclude. In his mind, the fundamental task in improving Connington School—and the one he simply couldn't avoid if he were serious about his responsibilities as a young principal—was nothing less than a wholesale reconfiguration of the teaching staff. As he put it, there simply weren't the right people on the bus," and he foresaw no way through the deflection, avoidance, and plain lack of skills in the classroom than to attempt to replace large numbers of teachers. In fact, he saw something of a mandate in his quest to reconstitute the staff of the school. "I know that I've had the support of my bosses in doing what I need to do, to at least put the right players in place. And I think that at some level, there's an allowance there. But sometimes, people don't get why you lost six people last year. 'What was that about? There must be something you're doing that's turning people off.' I was like, 'Oh really? Because the year before, I lost about fourteen. The year before that, I lost about sixteen, and I was applauded for it.'"

In Huntington, like any other locality in Massachusetts, there was no straightforward way to remove a teacher from a position, even in the face of overwhelming evidence that he or she was ineffective. There was a system for transferring teachers against their will—what the city called involuntary transfers—but this was mainly reserved for teacher cuts for budgetary reasons or for problems of gross negligence. Teachers could also elect to transfer from their current position into any other school in the city of Huntington, with a minimum level of interference from principals in either the sending or the receiving school. Because Huntington was a large school system, there were frequent opportunities for voluntary transfers—provided that teachers found this preferable to the prospects of staying put. Consequently, with respect to hiring and firing, Martinez enjoyed no special advantage in having taken over the helm of a school in corrective action. Instead, he introduced a much greater level of accountability to Connington and willingly tolerated several years of immense dissatisfaction among many of his teachers; his ultimate intent was that they seek transfer from his school. "Yeah, I'd take people out," Martinez conceded. "But . . . I'm here in the field—at the ground level. And I need to think about how that's done. You know, starting with a way that doesn't have everybody looking over their shoulder, [I had to] try to control the climate at the same time."

The effects of this approach at Connington were clearly profound, even if Martinez was ultimately trying to find a new teaching force for the school. In the view of many current staff members, the exodus of so many veteran teachers from the school affected its culture—and not always in positive ways. "The turnover is tough," said Jimmie Stanzer. "Even just this last year, there are seven or eight new teachers. And there were five last year, and none of those five new teachers came back . . . I think it's hard to be consistent and really get something rolling if every year, a quarter or maybe an eighth of the staff is learning it new again." There was frustration in Stanzer's comment, and he obviously felt that the quality of his work—which he defined at least in part in terms of the progress of his teaching team and the entire school—was made more challenging by the cycle of new teachers arriving and other teachers departing unexpectedly. "Those bumps keep popping back up [each year] because it's not the same team," Stanzer continued. "Jill Prescott and I are the only two that have been the same for two years, which is really interesting to me, because we've worked with three of the four different other fourth-grade teachers. Some of them don't know the curriculum; some of them are new to this age level."

"A lot of people use Connington as a stepping-ground to get into the Huntington school system," Stanzer elaborated. "It seems there are always one or two teachers every year from each grade level that leave . . . Unfortunately, you don't know that until August, when we come back from the summer and learn, oh, Ms. So-and-So is not coming back . . . And then there are three new faces. They're young, they're new, which can be a good thing because then you kind of have that attitude, 'I want to be told what to do.' But then sometimes there are older teachers that have been teaching for a long time, and they think they have it all, but some of it is different from what the school wants. It's tough." Stanzer tried not to be discouraged by this, but there was clearly a sense of confusion about the ongoing changes, and he said that he was left with a lingering question about how long the staff instability would continue.

To be fair, most teachers' comments about the massive turnover at Connington tended to be positive; they described the shift in the teaching staff—mainly from longtime Huntington veterans to mostly young teachers in the first five years of their careers—as an influential step for the school. In general, they noted that the attitude of the staff had changed, that teachers had now "gotten it," and that they no longer felt that they were working against the professional norms of the school when they participated in meetings or discussed the needs of their students in terms of their own teaching.

As much as they facilitated a different overall tone in the building, these new teachers brought their own challenges, and Martinez could not ignore these new, annual costs. "You know, each September, it's like we have to take a couple steps back because we've got to bring the new teachers up to speed. And things aren't as tight as I like them to be, and I hope they may be again. In February and March, the little things like routines [that still aren't working] just have me pulling my hair out. But they just need the time," he told himself. "Just be patient, and let people kind of work on their repertoire a little bit."

For Aaron Carpenter, a twenty-three-year-old graduate of Boston College and one of many teachers new to the school in the 2007 school year, Connington was a harsh place to start a career. Like Martinez, he was aware of how much he'd had to struggle just to master the basics of classroom management, instructional routines, and curriculum. Martinez's patience for Carpenter's learning was a mixed blessing, especially in his first year, when the young man felt his teaching was going so poorly that he questioned his decision to enter the field at all. Now into his second year of teaching, Carpenter described his first year at Connington with an evident strain: "I felt like an awful teacher. I would come home from work emotionally drained . . . I felt like I was killing myself, struggling with these kids. There were twenty-one kids I was responsible for, and I just felt like I knew nothing about education. I felt like I wasn't prepared to teach."

From the comments of all these Connington teachers about the effects of the battles between veteran teachers and the principal, the exodus of so many teachers from the school, and the yearly struggles of handfuls of young teachers to replace them, a different picture of the school began to emerge. Clearly, Martinez had a full plate in his first few years: several of his staff described a very active and belligerent union presence at the school during his first four years, and the hiring of so many teachers each year was surely a massive drain of his time and energy. His ability to support his teachers, especially as they came in the door younger and less experienced, was apparently very limited. If Carpenter's experiences were indicative, many of the youngest teachers at the Connington would have experienced a fair degree of isolation through these years. In the face of such difficult working conditions—with a challenging student body, a largely discontented staff, and a determined, if overly busy principal—some chose to leave, while others were not invited to return, and Martinez was faced with their replacement as well. Teams of teachers were difficult to form, and even a basic sense of camaraderie was hard in coming. After five years of effort to reconstitute the staff, teachers at the Connington may have wanted to participate in the school's betterment, but many were still mightily consumed by their classroom duties, and others were struggling with exactly how they should plug into schoolwide improvement projects. The turnover may have been essential to the school—there may been no way to convert the roster of teachers that Martinez found when he began as principal into what he thought of a "team that could make the playoffs"—but the tactic brought its own costs. And coupled with the added costs of so great a tightening of control at the school, Connington was still facing a good number of daunting challenges.

If staff turnover defined one important aspect of the school's trajectory in the wake of its declaration as an underperforming school, the dramatic increase in the direction of curricula, assessment, and teaching techniques by the school's principal and assistant principal defined another. Connington teachers said that during the school's evolution in this regard, nearly every aspect of the school's programming—from students' classroom groupings to deadlines for unit assessments in each subject area—came under the direct control of Martinez in the first two years of his tenure. Meeting agendas were similarly dictated by the principal, as were common classroom procedures and teaching strategies. In a very short time, Connington went from a place of minimal direction—where teachers were, in essence, free to run their classrooms as they saw fit—to one of tight central control. The impetus for this change was clearly the school's restructuring status, but how this change was pursued came purely from Martinez.

All the teachers I spoke with pointed to one particular incident as the most powerful—and damaging—event related to this striking shift in control at Connington. The school's instructional leadership team had created a checklist to measure the implementation of some key strategies from an early version of the school's improvement plan. According to Jessica Hereford, Martinez had approached the members of the team about creating the checklist, and they had seen a certain sense in devising a method for systematically observing and collecting data about classroom practice at Connington. When the checklist was used, though—by Martinez on his own, in unannounced visits to classrooms and evidently as part of his evaluation of teachers—it sparked a massive controversy at the school. Hereford explained what happened: "[The checklist] made sense to me—that you need to measure [classroom teaching] . . . But then a lot of the other teachers in the leadership team had a hard time . . . because it got implemented in more of a punitive way than in a data-gathering way. It didn't seem to be something that we were using for our growth and understanding. It seemed to be a way of ranking teachers and . . . giving negative feedback. Part of that was perception, . . . and part of it was reality. Part of it was reflecting badly on the teacher, and that was hard to see because I think the goal of it was good and useful. How it got used wasn't always [useful]—and that was frustrating."

"There were a lot of people complaining to the union about being asked to do things that they didn't feel were in their contract," recalled Hereford. She said that many staff members were very nearly in the throes of revolt: "There was a lot of data collection, and there still is a lot of data collection. But it seemed like an extraordinary amount in our first two years . . . There were a lot of the things about posting objectives, a lot of things about lesson plan books . . . People felt very disempowered . . . And so the only way they felt that they could wield any power over what was going on was to involve the union and to push back in that way. It seemed like having a constructive conversation with anybody wasn't possible. So, it became just refusal. 'I'm not going to do it, and I don't have to, and you can't make me.'" Hereford concluded that nothing about what Martinez wanted was, in itself, unreasonable to the teachers then at the school; it was simply how the new requirements were presented. In her estimate, the resistance was "a matter of principle" about how teachers would be treated at the Connington, and it included almost every teacher at the school at the time.

Not every new project at Connington had the same result as the flap about the checklist, though. Although Martinez finally withdrew the checklist from use, a great many other initiatives took flight during the early years of his principalship. It was an impressive list, which, in Martinez's estimate, exactly matched the vision of the school district's ten-year reform effort.

In recent years, teachers routinely posted the objectives of their lessons and were organized to deliver the three-tiered reading intervention that was part of the school's Reading First initiative. The submission of formative assessment data—from monthly tests in reading, writing, and mathematics—was now routine, and teachers regularly received electronic readouts of these results from across the school. Instructional coaches were active across the school; the SEI program became more and more articulated. Every teacher with whom I spoke, and Martinez himself, was contented with the overall fidelity of the implementation of the math and reading programs. As Martinez pointed out, Connington recently received high marks from the deputy superintendent during a recent visit, particularly in the area of program fidelity. Connington was one of a handful of "model" schools in the city, and Martinez was promoted to the position of principal prefect, serving other elementary principals in his neighborhood as a mentor and coach, on the basis of his exemplary instructional leadership.

Martinez also seemed especially effective reaching out to members of the Connington community and generating additional funds for the school to establish programs he felt would benefit his students. At a time when Huntington students were losing many extracurricular opportunities because of a diminishing city budget, Martinez successfully convinced a dozen or so local musicians to begin offering instrumental music lessons to the school's upper-grade students and secured a sizable grant to purchase instruments and pay his instructors. He refurbished the school's faded library with help from a local congregation and, in his largest effort, won grant funding for a multiyear project with a nearby community health agency to provide on-site mental health counseling to individuals and groups of students during the school day. On one of the days I toured the school with him, he proudly pointed out a massive, new world map and multicolored running track that he and community volunteers had painted onto Connington's cracked asphalt playground that same weekend.

In part, Martinez was able to accomplish these things—even in the face of considerable dissent from many teachers—because he looked to a few similarly minded teachers to carry forward his agenda. The school's leadership team, which the city had established in every city school when Martinez was still a Spanish bilingual teacher in another part of town, was Connington's official vehicle for change. Consequently, important improvement work, like the creation of the school improvement plan, was supposed to run through the team. Martinez found five teachers in these early years to sit on the team, and at least for several years, all the school's data analysis, planning, and product formation came from this group. This early leadership team—dubbed the "Fab Five" by other teachers, who viewed the team as the principal's own chosen ones—had created the classroom checklist that was so offensive to other teachers.

The team continued to cause resentment among the other teachers— or at least a sense of team isolation from them. For Jimmie Stanzer, a member of the Fab Five, this sense of exclusion by other teachers and the fear of speaking openly in front of Martinez diminished the quality of Connington's professional conversations. "Sometimes, there's a lot of confusion around the MCAS, and [people wonder] 'What does it really mean, and what's really going to happen to us?' People are afraid to talk about it. Even today, when the principal gave us [new MCAS data], he came in and talked to the group, and you could just see people putting their heads down."

Hereford, on the other hand, viewed this phenomenon of teachers' fear not as a function of a personal difference between teachers and their principal, but as a direct consequence of the period in which Martinez exercised such tight control over nearly every aspect of the school.

For her, it was a matter of trust; she believed that her colleagues were justified in doubting the extent of Martinez's intentions to share leadership of the school. "I think because it was so top-down for my first two years here, now when it's supposed to be more bottom-up, people don't trust it. [Teachers have] this thought that they're going to do this work, work on that improvement plan, think about measurement tools and all that stuff, only in the end to have somebody say, 'No, that's not what we're doing. This is what we have to do, something else entirely'—and nobody wants to engage in that work if it's not going to be honored in the end."

Hereford believed that Connington was in a peculiar bind at this stage of its development. The resistant teachers were mostly gone, and in their place was a combination of midcareer teachers with highly refined skill sets, each hired for a demonstrated competence and for aspirations of teacher leadership, and young teachers still working to master the most basic aspects of classroom teaching. The school pursued a very organized reform agenda—in which the Reading First grant and its many requirements for classroom teaching, school structure, student groupings, and interventions played a central part—and these requirements continued to exist. There was heavy school lore about teachers being driven out of the building by a rigorous, if somewhat aloof, principal, and some teachers still felt hounded by his expectations. The strategies had largely been about fidelity of implementation and the uniformity of each classroom in the school. For the school's most skilled educators, the ones recruited for their talent and knowledge, there were considerable restrictions on what was possible in the classroom, and they were not sure how to agitate for changes in classroom instruction. For the younger set, the tight guidance around curriculum was welcome; as Aaron Carpenter said, it was great to be "told what to do." Teacher leadership, which Martinez could he'd always valued and which he viewed as the key to Connington's success, appeared to be hugely subject to this dilemma: central control, as an initial response to a staff of limited competence and commitment, was necessary; now that the staff was so different, this level of control, even if it was only perceived by teachers, was incredibly hard to undo.

Principal Martinez was aware of this dilemma about undoing the effects of the tight control on teachers' creativity and leadership, though he might not have entirely perceive its depth. "In the early years, I was the one facilitating and planning and running every meeting in this building, whether it was a student support team or the leadership team or whatever it was. If there were more than two people there, I was there, too." He had a handle on as much as he could, he said, because he had no choice. It was a choice between giving direction or accepting that there would be none at all. The difference was that now, the team had some experience under its belt. "This is the team that I want," he said, "the team who's going to pull it off. So I want to make sure and come off as supportive and trusting of their capabilities. And oftentimes, you know, that might even come off as a little bit of inattentiveness or nonchalance, . . . in giving them the space to do what . . . they know how to do well. Another thing I've learned is not to micromanage everybody in the building, because I know that they're very competent, sometimes, in what they do."

Hesitations aside, Martinez now imagined a school in which a robust, informed debate about best practice was possible—and free of the inhibitions of the past: "[I tell teachers] 'If you can justify for me where your kids are at, what you know they need this week or this month, and you're going to pull from [resources other than the school's programs], go for it. I trust your professional judgment, I trust your expertise.'" He added, "And so sometimes I have to say that a little bit more explicitly to people—to people who seem to think we do things because there's a clipboard walking around, and not because it's the right thing to do."

For Hereford, one issue that particularly exemplified the dilemma of central control and teacher leadership was literacy, specifically the way the school had to implement the prescriptions of the Reading First grant. Historically, Connington had struggled mightily with its English language arts scores, and for the eight years that the school had some form of accountability label, Connington had never met its AYP goals in reading.

Reading First brought the school a significant amount of money and, according to Martinez, satisfied the DOE's requirement that the school have a well-formulated plan for improvement. The department also stipulated that the school adopt a reading program with empirical evidence of effectiveness and that the school structure a rigorous program of intervention for the lowest-performing students. To do this, Connington adopted a new, more scripted reading program, instituted the collection of literacy data, and had its reading specialists adopt pull-out-style intervention. These changes effectively replaced a longstanding citywide effort to encourage teachers, including those at Connington, to use reading and writing workshop as a primary method for the instruction of literacy.

The workshop approach heavily emphasized teachers' knowledge of reading development, particularly in the areas of reading for comprehension and metacognitive strategies. At the time, Martinez believed that workshops represented too challenging an instructional model for the Connington staff he encountered when he was hired. Besides, unlike the workshop model in other city schools, the model had never been well supported with any sustained professional development for teachers, and there was little opportunity for any meaningful support at that point.

The new reading program contained all the components of the workshop approach—like small-group instruction, frequent assessment, writing prompts, and strategy instruction—but in a much more accessible format and with a well-laid-out sequence and pace. With weekly units and daily lesson plans, the program was a good deal different from the month-long "trajectories" that teachers were expected to craft on their own in the workshop model. At the time, Martinez said, Reading First and the new, scripted reading program made good sense for the school, and he insisted over the next few years that both approaches be implemented faithfully and in every classroom.

Harford explained the problem with this strategy: "In the first few years that we were implementing the scripted reading program, the message was being sent clearly that you needed to be true to the program and there was no teacher judgment involved. You do what you are told, and that's how it's going to be." The problem, she insisted, was that the results weren't showing up—either on the MCAS or on the DIBELS

(Dynamic Indicators of Basic Early Literacy Skills)—and that some of her best ways of teaching, like reading strategy instruction, were things that she wasn't allowed to do. "They were very clear that you weren't supposed to stray from it in any way, shape, or form—to the point of getting any other books out of the room."

Cheryl Simms, in her second year of teaching kindergarten at Connington, described a similar pressure to adhere strictly to the lesson plans she was provided in the new reading program. "Well, with interventions, [they say] this is the curriculum we're using for interventions. In my old school, I did it differently; I created the lesson plans. I see definitely where it's good to have more common ground, but there are skills that I would like to give—more authentic learning. That's what I miss here, and I think that's where the AYP comes in. It's with all the tests and all the curriculum mandates . . . you feel like you just don't have time, because you're ninety minutes here, sixty minutes here." Simms felt that the tone of the school was shifting this year, but there was still much uncertainty about exactly how much latitude she could expect from the school's leaders. She was like many other teachers in saying this; despite the hardships of the past years, it was this present school year that felt the most promising. There was a palpable shift in the school, and nearly everyone—even with the devastating MCAS results then coming in—saw more possibilities for the future.

Stanzer succinctly summed up what he saw: it was all about the staff's finally having a sense of accountability—not to the state or the district or even to the principal. Though the development was recent and still shaky, they had discovered a sense of accountability to one another. "There seems to be more of a consistent approach to professionalism. This is the first year. You know, accountability, getting stuff done. We say we're going to do this; now let's get it done."

State and Local Interventions at Connington School

At Stoddard and Tanner Schools, where teachers and principals struggled to make sense of relatively new accountability labels (Stoddard was declared a school in corrective action in 2004 and was one of the first in the commonwealth; Tanner was called a school in need of improvement in the fall of 2007), there were frequent complaints about the overwhelming sense of isolation that accompanied this status. P. T. Coelho, the Stoddard PIM facilitator, had the advantage of state training in PIM, but otherwise felt that he and Ken Schumer, his new principal, were left to figure out what to do to improve Stoddard's flagging MCAS scores. At Tanner K–8 in Hoover, Principal Trisha Waighn felt that she was facing the state's requirements and the scrutiny of her veteran staff completely on her own. A sense of aloneness was evidently one of the hallmarks in the experience of these underperforming schools.

At Connington, this pattern in the faculty's and administrators' perception persisted—even after eight years of school restructuring, and in a school district with a national reputation for thoughtful school reform. On this count, in fact, Martinez was at his most indignant. "There should have been intervention after year two," he scoffed. "The intervention has been my additional eighteen hours of work a week, that's it. It's just not helpful to me to have a draft plan for ways central office or the state is going to support us—potentially—for the school next year. I'll continue to ask for what you can help me with tomorrow."

The state was not uninvolved at the Connington, but its involvement changed radically after the first few years, particularly as the DOE reworked its school review and intervention processes in 2006.[1] In 2004, the state's panel review team was largely complimentary of Connington's efforts to analyze its MCAS data, involve teachers in leadership opportunities, and engage the staff in meaningful professional development. The reviewers, however, did fault the school for several vaguely worded goals and some superficial data analysis with respect to student subgroups. The 2004 review constituted the majority of the feedback the school had received from the state; in fact, since the publication of the report by the state panel, Connington hasn't been the subject of any state inquiry or action.

In light of the various state interventions at Connington, such as the panel review and the state's pending Priority Schools legislation, Martinez was, understandably, unsure on what he stood to gain in any arrangement with the state. In his eyes, there was not much in the Priority Schools designation that he didn't already have. He'd weathered the storm to replace the majority of his staff, and in 2007 he had created a new leadership structure in which every teacher in the school was involved. He had three coaches already. What he wanted was new ideas—a new set of strategies that evidence suggests would result in something other than the decline of his students' scores. Or, he said, he just wanted to know that he could move on the ideas he already had.

What Went Wrong at Connington School: Four Common Avoidable Mistakes

Like the situation with Stoddard and Tanner Schools, patterns in the details of Connington suggest several lessons for improving schools. First, there is no way to consider Connington without understanding the effect of teachers' discontent and turnover over such a long period. (One suspects that the same situation could easily have occurred at either Stoddard or Tanner with a principal as hard-charging as Martinez; in fact, the staff "veto" at Connington was something that Stoddard and Tanner people said they feared—and they acted to avoid this calamity.) Second, Connington was hard-pressed for new ideas, especially in light of the educators' belief that they had actually realized the set of goals they had established in their early years of restructuring. This absence of any obvious and accessible source of expertise for the school bears further thought. Finally, Connington raised important questions about the impact of state and district policies on the school's continuing poor performance.

High Teacher Turnover and Little Teacher Accountability

There's a remarkable parallel between all three schools in the makeup of their faculties in the years preceding a designation as underperforming by the state. At Connington School, like Tanner and Stoddard, the composition of the staff had been something of a constant; teachers rarely sought out transfers to other schools, and when there was a resignation, they left Connington mainly for personal reasons. In the first years of Connington's designation as an underperforming school, and not co-incidentally during the first years of Jesse Martinez's tenure as principal, this stability began to erode. For years, Martinez was Connington's iconoclast, printing lists of what he expected to see from his teachers and then going into classrooms to observe, give feedback, and confront. He apparently accepted that the school would be rocked backward—even knocked to the ground—so that it could walk in the future.

One significant by-product of this tactic was that Connington now appeared to be locked into a cycle of high teacher turnover and that any gains from increased teachers' sense of responsibility would be offset by the half-dozen inexperienced recruits who filled a quarter of the school's classrooms each year. Without any changes to the existing operation, these young teachers began their careers in a school that still required great proficiency in redirecting demanding student behavior. Meanwhile, these new teachers, who were only beginning to connect to their grade-level teams, had to face a school with only an incipient sense of schoolwide cohesion and a principal's nearly hands-off approach to praising his teachers. It was not a formula for high retention. Add to this that Connington was subject to young teachers' career decisions in the same way that any other school is—new teachers typically view their commitment to the education profession as something like five years of service—and it was hard to see how the school would stanch its current level of turnover.[2]

Apart from the impact of young teachers on individual classrooms, their inexperience was also felt around the school. At meetings, they were described as mostly quiet or "overwhelmed by the content" of discussions about data and teaching strategy, mainly because nearly everything was new to them. By the same token, schoolwide routines were hard to maintain with so many new teachers, a situation that Martinez lamented. He said that even in the previous year, "[I was] pulling my hair out about simple things that should be solid in February and March." Clearly, there's more to school improvement than the can-do attitude that comes with youth; a healthy dose of can-do skill is every bit as important. And at the Connington, this skill was more abundant than ever before. But it was still not universal, and the school was continually hampered by these weak spots, just as it had been in years past.

The meetings that Stanzer described—where some teachers felt fear, others were embarrassed or overwhelmed about what they didn't know, and still others were confused about their role after a defining period of tight central control—were vitally important to Connington. In Martinez's view, they represented the way forward. These meetings couldn't any longer be about conveying information and expectations from the top to the bottom. Martinez knew that he had to right the ship in his first years and that this took a strong hand. He also knew that the ship couldn't be piloted successfully without the best effort—and best thinking—of its crew. He needed more experts at his school. He needed what he called a professional learning community.

Martinez believed that his teachers held the keys to the school's success. The winning combination, he argued—and what he had been working toward in every agonizing year of his tenure—consisted of solid infrastructures for collecting and analyzing data, sharing successes among teachers, and supporting teachers to learn new classroom methods. Couple these things with compelling norms of collegiality and uniform implementation, and the Connington would have a chance. The system he wanted to build was decidedly not about control and compliance, which he initially felt compelled to pursue in the face of so disproportionate a level of disinterest and resistance. It was about teacher autonomy and professionalism, but of a different sort than what he first encountered at his school. This autonomy was not about teachers closing their classroom doors to pursue their own stylistic leanings. Martinez's version of autonomy had to do with leveraging teachers' skills and experience to find and spread what the data suggested would work well for children. It's the part about basing decisions on evidence that made the model so different.

Inadequate Professional Development

In the end, Martinez realized that the strictures of the new scripted reading program didn't hold enough promise for literacy acquisition at

Connington. Nor could the guidelines of the Reading First grant be ad-
hered to year after year—mainly because neither effort garnered any
significant growth in achievement. He described his decision to pursue
these initiatives: "I liked the professional development, the very specific
time spent talking about components of reading. You know, [for] our
core program, it would provide materials, consistency across classrooms.
Was this a bad thing? And, at the same time, we needed to have a clearer
strategy for addressing our ELA and AYP shortcomings." But now, he
said, the imperative was different: "I've now got a hundred percent of my
staff signed on, and we're implementing to a high degree of fidelity. Why,
then, am I not getting the results that you said that I would get? And
point out to me a school in the commonwealth that is getting them."

Martinez elaborated about this shift: "When teachers get to the point
where they say, 'You know, we really need thirty minutes a day spent on
X, Y, Z, and then we try it, and we learn if it works, and then that problem is resolved. As a group, that's what we need to do now." So, Martinez reasoned, there was a new direction in store for Connington—a
new stage in its internal workings. Autonomy, controlled experimenta-
tion in teaching practice, and evidence-based professional learning were
the order of the day.

Little Systemic Support for Innovation

In some respects, there was no other option for Connington School to pursue, other than to simply rest on the satisfaction that teachers were doing
what they were supposed to. But this has never been the premise of standards-based reform, and everyone I talked to at the Connington knew it.
At the end of the day, kids need to demonstrate what they've learned. The
next logical question, though—and the next challenge that the school
had to resolve—was where the expertise for sustained professional learning would come from. If the scripted reading wasn't working, if Reading
First and its three tiers of intervention had so far been insufficient, if the
reading and writing workshop model had gone underground—then what
would be the next big idea that the school would pursue? And how would
this idea surface? Where would it come from?

Assuming no major changes in the role played so far by the central office or the state DOE, there were only a few available answers to this question. First, the teachers with whom I spoke placed a premium on their own ability to generate new ideas through reading and independent research. They talked about their own reading of literacy writers like Lucy Calkins or recent articles about a group of schools known as "90-90-90 schools," where local educators had succeeded in dramatically raising test scores in the face of poverty and disadvantage. Several teachers at Connington talked about the utility of two district-level reading specialists who were assigned to the school several years earlier, and credited the pair with helping them implement the scripted reading program and serve the needs of special education students in the classroom. Though the specialists were now reassigned, Connington teachers said that they were open to this type of feedback from district experts and hoped for some additional infusion of knowledge in the near future. Also mentioned was the school's student support team, the team of teachers required of all schools for the purpose of assisting students with disabilities in their regular education settings. The teachers trusted that, working with the team, teachers could brainstorm new solutions to the persistent behavioral and learning problems they encountered each year. A few other teachers were optimistic about the signals from their principal that the school would now be more open to classroom activities that fell outside the plans in the school's official programs. Kindergarten teacher Jill Prescott hoped that her students wouldn't have to endure over two hours of explicit reading instruction each day and she could return to what she considered the staples of her teaching before she was recruited to Connington: field trips to local sites of interest for the purpose of enrichment and building general knowledge, hands-on projects like baking pies, and more celebrations to better develop her students' pride in their school and enjoyment of their learning.

Like Martinez, the teachers were now focused intently on the prospects of their new, enhanced structures for teaming. "We're all asking, am I doing enough?" said Cheryl Simms. "People really need to step up with ideas and then move those ideas forward and really follow through and implement. [We need to] brainstorm new ways and really get into, not just test score data and what our score needs are, but what our classroom needs are and how we can use our colleagues."

If there was a random quality to these thoughts—that after eight years of serious, pressurized work, a new idea from the staff would spark the turnaround they'd all waited for—at least some teachers at Connington appeared to be aware of it. Hereford saw that the school had entered a new period in its efforts, one that she somewhat cynically referred to as the stage of serendipity:

Martinez had similar thoughts about where the next big idea at the Connington would come from. As he put it, he was just a step ahead of the staff in thinking about what would come next for the school—and this, he reminded me, put him well ahead of the district and the state. "Well, I'm always trying to think about what we could do—a little vision for what next—what next—and I spend a lot of energy lobbying to make those things a reality, whether it's resources or enough money or new people. I can see a portion of the staff beginning to feel that way, like, 'Okay, we've done all these things. We've gone above and beyond. But instead of showing me a bump in improvement, we're going the other direction.' That's frustrating for me to feel that. You know, we're stalling in that respect."

In the juxtaposition of the school's need for teacher leadership and innovation and the legacy of so much firm control from the office, Connington's dilemma appeared most pronounced. No longer fighting about the question of will, it was twisting mightily about what it should do now.

More than Tanner and Stoddard Schools, Connington had passed through a few distinct stages over the previous eight years. There were the early fights about responsibility, common expectations for teachers, and accountability to authority—whether that authority was the staff or the principal. This period gave way to new work centered on uniform implementation, hiring, and the creation of collaborative structures. Now, Connington was developing a new ethic of professionalism and empiricism—even if a substantial number of its youngest staff members were finding their initiation to the school to be a rocky affair. Each stage was unique, and each seemed logically to stem from the one that preceded it.

To a lesser degree, Connington was also unique in the series of emotional and cognitive stages that the staff experienced. It was obvious to a visitor that the Connington's teachers were shocked and discouraged by their students' most recent performance on the MCAS. In one way, it was an identical reaction to the one current Connington veterans described about the school's first designation as an underperforming school. Eight years later, it was a different group of teachers and students, but the news was no less disheartening. The reaction was essentially the same one gripping Tanner School: teachers just couldn't believe the scores; there was too large a disconnect between their sense that they worked hard and their students' results on the exam.

In the earliest stage of Connington's identity as an underperforming school, there was a fair amount of thinking about external causes of student failure. At the time, teachers pointed to low levels of English language use in many homes, relatively poor support for school policy among families, and the pulverizing effects of poverty on many families. These were widely acknowledged as the true causes of the school's weak performance. In Martinez's eyes, this was simple deflection, and his staff purges were intended to rid the school of this attitude. Paradoxically, then, a new round of thinking about what was going on outside Covington might have been hindering efforts to improve. Though probably not an act of deflection, it did represent a return of the idea that there were some things that the school couldn't control—and that these things actually mattered. It suggested, too, that there were cycles in the school's development—that some things kept coming up—even as the school passed through a series of linear stages.

Reversion to Blaming Externalities

At Connington in 2007, the new version of the familiar thought that outside circumstances contributed significantly to students' weak performance centered on how the Huntington school district was set up. That is, the faculty was beginning to wonder if teachers were not the only ones responsible for what was going on, then maybe the school department's bureaucracy warranted some examination as well.

Not surprisingly, Martinez had the most to say about this, though many of his teachers made similar points. The principal was in the best position to interact frequently with district-level administrators, and after working in Huntington since 1997, Martinez was the most familiar with the district's policies. He referred to bureaucratic problems as systemic barriers, and he wondered how he was supposed to coach his team to victory when the playing field was so skewed to his disadvantage. At its most gentle, Martinez's criticism acknowledged the steep learning curve that district administrators had to climb as they created a comprehensive, standards-based reform model in the late 1990s. During this period, the direction from the district was important, but perfunctory. "'You'll be doing [reading and writing] workshops,'" he said, paraphrasing the district's direction at the time. "'You'll be having an instruction leadership team; there'll be some kind of an improvement plan that each school should have crafted.' At the time, there wasn't a heavy emphasis on understanding or on working with data. They knew that it needed to be rooted in data, but even back then, the district was kind of new at this. [They eventually] realized we should stop this business of annual planning and go to at least a multiyear plan. They provided the prerequisites for what the school should have going on. But what it meant activity-wise, the quality and the depth weren't there." In Martinez's view, the district never got to this next stage in its thinking, and by 2007, issues related to the quality of interventions were still entirely his to sort out.

Martinez focused next on the transience of Connington's student population, and though he was aware of the complicated factors that contribute to the school's 36 percent mobility rate, he also considered aspects of the district's student assignment policy problematic for his school. As he asked, why shouldn't the city leverage its size—and the fact that there are a handful of more successful, more stable elementary schools in his geographical zone—to the advantage of its most needy schools? Why couldn't the steady, yearlong flow of students from other cities and countries be better distributed or entirely redirected at some point in the school year, to help the Connington stay focused? "Just close the gates," he said, "so at least [the students] I have are the ones I'm going to have. It would make a difference. There's a group of schools in this same predicament right now—ones that are moving into this Commonwealth Priority Schools phase. At least provide relief right now on capping our enrollment."

Martinez thought that the district could have at least considered the issue of class size as well. "I think if we just have a little relief here through attrition, to bring down the numbers [of students] a little bit, it would help to have stability here. You look at the higher-performing schools on this side of town, and the ones where ninety percent of the stable students are also high performing. They're also the schools that have very low free- or reduced-lunch rates. So let the school down the street have some of our kids. They're ninety-five percent stable." The same could go for student disciplinary transfers, he asserted. He described it as an effort to protect the school from potential sources of instability and to better distribute the city's collective burdens.

There were other policy decisions, too, that had given Martinez pause over the years. He was convinced that the addition of more classes to the school's sheltered English instruction and self-contained special education programs lowered the school's scores and that it didn't make sense to concentrate the challenges that came with these programs in a single, already-underperforming school. In a way, he viewed it as the odd product of his success. "We've worked hard [with the self-contained and SEI programs], but we made a kind of an incentive for the district [to say], 'So let's send the Connington fifty-one more English language learners to figure out what they can do with them—because we don't have the plan as a district, but they do.' And then they also say, 'Well, let's designate the school as a self-contained program; let's assign kids from all over the city, on an ongoing basis. They've kind of articulated a program out there for special education students with behavioral challenges, so let's fill them up over there.' So, you're a school in restructuring, and yet the district just doesn't need it as a [small, neighborhood] home school." Add to this a chaotic student assignment and transportation system, in which many of Connington's closest students, who reside in recently constructed luxury condominiums, boarded buses each morning for schools in more privileged sections of the city, and the school seemed destined for problems. "You know," Martinez concluded, "you have to ask if the system's policies over time haven't naturally resulted in where we're at."

As a case in point, Martinez pointed to a single district-level decision the previous year and its disastrous consequences for his MCAS scores. At the beginning of the year, Martinez learned that he would have to accept a new teacher to the Connington, one who he heard was being administratively reassigned for misconduct in the teacher's last school. "He was assigned from the central office, as a brand new sheltered English teacher [for me] to work with. He didn't make it past Christmas with me, but it created a lot of inconsistency. We had to pull someone else [out of another assignment] until we found somebody to carry it out the rest of the year." So, during the several-month period leading up to the March administration of the MCAS, the school's MCAS preparation specialist was assigned to this vacated classroom, and the services she provided—particularly to upper-grade students—were discontinued. "The whole thing shows in our test scores, because the kids bombed. You look at our MCAS scores, and you see that our ELL kids didn't do well in grades four and five. It wasn't a surprise."

Finally, the Connington principal was especially indignant about the city's Advanced Work program, which he considered a form of robbery. Martinez was hard-pressed to imagine how his school would improve its aggregate scores without some change to this long-standing program. In the Huntington district, examination schools are elite, public middle schools and high schools that accept students from every quarter of the city on the basis of their test scores and grades. Starting in the fourth grade, the highest-performing students from every school in Huntington, including Connington, are invited to attend special advanced-work programs scattered about the city in a few select schools. These students often matriculate into one of a few prestigious examination high schools.

Every year, Connington loses the majority of its most able fourth- and fifth-grade students to this program—something on the order of about a quarter to a third of each class—and their seats are filled by incoming, usually lower-performing students. It was another way, Martinez insisted, that the deck was stacked against him, and another way that the Connington was unnecessarily disadvantaged in its struggle to achieve proficiency. In all these cases of "systemic barriers," Martinez's evolving view was that there was a limit to the countervailing effect of good instruction on systemic incoherence and that he could only do so much as a principal without a larger move to reexamine the way things had been done for years in the city.

At Connington School, there was clearly a sense that the formula they'd pursued for years needed to begin to work. The new staff, the relatively new programs, the management structure, and the attention to uniform implementation—all of these were the building blocks on which Martinez and his staff had built their aspirations for their school. Recently, though, they had been unable to improve the school's scores and had been languishing for many hard years in their status as a restructuring school. The unlikelihood that help would be on the way both quickened their resolve and added to their sense of isolation. They all continued to want desperately to make a difference—the critical difference, they hoped—at Connington; they were just no longer sure that they were doing the right things.

Another year or two in the same direction might have been sufficient to tell if there was real promise in the school's development of its own capacity—of its internal accountability. Teachers might have struck upon strategies that worked and brought these new strategies to scale. They might also have encountered another set of tough problems, which could have caused more delays to their upward trajectory. By the same token, the team at Connington was changing every year, and the school might have continued to experience so much change in its staff that sustained attention to the same strategies—and sustained improvement in student achievement—might never have been possible. Martinez could have burned out at the end of the year, and a new principal might have spent several more years plotting a new course. None of this could be easily predicted. And none of it—not the slow, painful crawl toward the teachers' sense of accountability or the accumulation of promising school practices—would correspond to the overly easy literature about school improvement. It was long, complicated work for the people at Connington, just as it had been for the staff members of Stoddard and Tanner Schools. None had been aware of any formula for success, and all had adapted in ways as unique as each of their situations.

Part 2

Understanding Intervention's Problems and Potential

CHAPTER

4

What's Going Wrong
with Intervention?

Obviously, the work that Stoddard, Tanner, and Connington were required to perform as part of their accountability status only accounted for a portion of what made these years so difficult for them. They did satisfy the Massachusetts Department of Education (DOE) requirements: they looked at their test scores, identified new strategies that they would implement, and considered for the first time what some form of internal inspection of their own work might look like. But these things took place against a significant backdrop of additional challenges that are also essential to understanding what was really happening in these schools. The technical requirements of being an underperforming school may have sparked these crises, but they provided no guidance about how they would be resolved. As they sought some resolution, the schools necessarily fell back on their default positions—to the personalities, relationships, and fragilities that defined them in the past.

The Tanner, Connington, and Stoddard Schools' technical responses to accountability also showed their struggle with isolation, the emotions of their faculties, and their homespun politics. The designs of the accountability system had gone awry. The schools were either stuck in place, given to the throes of local intrigues and anger, or locked into the same habits as before.

So, what went wrong with these interventions that so little appeared to be resetting in these target schools? And why are these schools' problems apparently so common—so emblematic of our ongoing challenge to improve education in our most vulnerable schools—even after a decade of testing, accountability, and intervention?

One answer to these questions is that state accountability systems have pretty well ignored how complicated low-performing schools can be, how different they are from one another. These schools vary greatly in how they improve, learn collaboratively, and establish mutual obligations; in their leadership; and in how they are affected, for better or worse, by the district. There's no single model for schools, and yet most states are banking on a decidedly one-model operation for their reform. Some astute observations about this variability have recently emerged and are worth investigating.

A second answer to these questions is that state accountability doesn't reset any of the foundational facts of low-performing schools. Intervention does nothing to remedy the grave, long-standing isolation that most of these schools experience. It fails to lessen the sources of instability inside low-performing schools, forcing school leaders who should be occupied with improvement to play a constant game of politics. Contract provisions about tenure and teaching assignments don't change when the state shows up. Nor do site politics just disappear. Principals and teachers aren't suddenly handed more time for collaboration, and they're not really in the position to undo their many decades of professional and intellectual isolation.

In reality, the stories from Stoddard, Tanner, and Connington suggest that state intervention, because it doesn't alter the lines in the rulebook, actually exacerbates the politics and isolation. The result, very obviously, was that the pressure increased inside these schools. In fact, the pressure to play politics is intense enough that the steps to improvement viewed as inexorable by state intervention theoreticians are actually experienced as dilemmas by schools, which wind up negotiating the steps in highly idiosyncratic ways. For example, the requirement that schools collect and analyze data, one hallmark of state intervention, doesn't necessarily lead to improved practice. It leads to new dilemmas and new balancing acts. Inside the school, the ways people resolve these dilemmas may actually make some sense to them. But with an eye on classroom-by-classroom improvements in teaching, the accretion of dozens of these small solutions can be nothing short of dysfunctional.

The third answer to what is going wrong with intervention is that intervention has so far placed a greater incentive on compliance than it has on professional learning and active problem-solving. Some schools, like the ones in this book, have found an odd comfort in following the directions they've been given—virtually to the point of passivity. New programs, new instructional materials, and new meetings have become a terminus of sorts, and some schools appear little inclined to see beyond these requirements to envision a larger, more proactive responsibility. Though the dynamic differed in each of the three schools in this book, the compliance orientation turned out to be a major problem, and all of them wound up stuck in its net.

This chapter gives space to these three answers to the question: What's going so wrong with intervention? To flesh out this answer, we begin by looking at research on the phenomenon of underperforming schools. From the stories of Stoddard, Tanner, and Connington, we will point out the most influential patterns in their day-to-day operation. In casting about for answers to this important question, we hope to find something new in the relationship between states and their underperforming schools. It's a way to say that something else is still missing—in fact, something new is urgently needed.

Low-Performing Schools Are More Complicated Than Expected

In recent years, a handful of scholars have attempted to understand the complex and novel interplay between states, districts, and schools—what Joan McRobbie has termed "the dilemma of the far extreme."[1]

One critical finding to emerge from this research is that not all underperforming schools are the same.[2] In fact, these schools vary in many ways, and these distinctions matter a great deal as the schools respond—both consciously and unconsciously—to the requirements of their state's intervention. Some of these variations are internal—like the extent to which teachers feel accountable to their colleagues for enacting a particular reform strategy—and others are external, like the degree to which their districts support the use of data by providing schools with the technical know-how needed to print reports and manipulate numbers. Only a few of these findings, however, are of such significance that they require any rewriting of intervention design. Moreover, only a few suggest that the complicated nature of underperforming schools really requires some serious rethinking on the part of leaders and policy makers. Four of these complications are described below.

First Complication: Nonlinear Improvement

One critical finding to emerge from the study of low-performing schools is Richard Elmore's description of the improvement process as nonlinear and characterized by occasional plateaus in student achievement and intermittent periods of outside assistance.[3] School improvement appears to begin in the way that state policy makers envision it, with schools making decisions based on data about student performance. Early decisions in school improvement, however, may be focused on interventions at the margins, either for groups of students at the cusp of a performance level or by emphasizing specific standards to immediately raise the school's accountability status.[4] Also during this first period, low-performing schools often attempt to intensify their current instructional practices, pursuing even more vigorously the same strategies that led to the poor performance they are now trying to correct [5] This intensification can include an emphasis on test-taking skills and increased remedial programming for at-risk students, all with the aim of achieving the short-term goal of restoring the school to its pre-intervention status. All of these activities are what researcher Heinrich Mintrop refers to as schools' "harvesting the low-hanging fruit."[6]

In addition, schools in the early stages of state-structured improvement also tend to experience increased central control by the principal and a heightened orientation toward compliance, which can lead to diminished satisfaction, increased staff turnover, and a diminution of the intrinsic rewards that research suggests are most important to teachers.[7] Surprisingly for schools under such close scrutiny, many low-performing schools become stuck, passing into a "competency trap," where teachers and administrators view only current and past practices as acceptable strategies for improvement.[8]

Largely on their own, many low-performing schools make wrong turns as they work to get better. Although these common maladaptive responses are well documented in the literature, there are surprisingly few accounts on low-performing schools' successful, adaptive responses to external accountability systems. In effect, researchers and educators provide little information about what a good response to accountability looks like—whether it's a description of roughly how long it takes to produce a meaningful turnaround under state sanction, or roughly what stages a school might pass through on its way to making steady, incremental gains, or which problems research has suggested are the right ones to solve. Of the few descriptions of these issues that are specific to low-performing schools in the throes of state accountability, two of them—one from Richard Elmore and the other from British researcher John Gray—warrant full description.

In 2003, Elmore proposed that school improvement is a process—one that should be acknowledged and supported by state officials concerned with the lowest-performing schools.[9] He described a sequence in which low-performing schools—the ones that are doing the right things, anyway—pass through a series of incrementally more challenging stages, where each stage is preceded by a period of stagnation in achievement and a sense of being overwhelmed. Schools with a growing internal capacity (the term Martin Carnoy and colleagues use for the complex combination of each individual's conception of professional responsibility, a school's collective expectations for student achievement and the quality of classroom instruction, and the school's formal accountability systems) and adequate external support manage to pass through these stalled periods, but only because they receive guidance from outside their ranks.[10] The existing capabilities of the staff are insufficient to accomplish the state's accountability goal of classroom-by-classroom improvements in teaching and learning. In the earliest stages of this process, low-performing schools frequently engage in work that is more related to compliance than any sustained examination of the effects of instruction on student achievement.[11] Instead, struggling schools will understandably pursue the "low-hanging fruit"—actions like aligning curriculum, identifying groups of low-performing students for targeted remediation, or making adjustments to the teaching schedule. Only later, after years of support with increasingly more challenging problems of student achievement, meaningful professional development, and the provision of external expertise, can low-performing schools be expected to possess the skills and orientation to become self-sustaining learning organizations. And it's this final state—in which schools possess a high level of internal capacity and exert expanding levels of professional competence to resolve more and more sophisticated problems of student learning—that represents the most promising goal for low-performing schools.

In the United Kingdom, British scholar John Gray developed a complementary description of schools that were deemed by the country's central inspectorate as underperforming.[12] Though observing schools a different country, Gray found that in general, low-performing schools in Britain also pass through a series of stages on their way to adequate performance. Typically, in the wake of an announcement by the government that they had not met some set of performance criteria, these schools first passed through a "time of crisis" in which the staff had to renew its commitment to changing established practices, to endure the uncertainty of restaffing, and to rethink the aspects of the school's context that may have served as excuses for poor performance in the past. During this first period, low-performing schools in Gray's study focused their attention on things that had little to do with the quality of teaching and learning: school schedules, student attendance, and the documentary requirements of the state's performance review. In particular, successful schools passed through this first period having developed an expanded set of leadership skills among both administrators and teachers, as well as substantive relationships with external support providers. As the schools progressed toward meaningful improvement, they developed a concern for the quality of teaching and professional development—a second, unique stage in their trajectory. This stage was characterized by school walk-throughs that began to focus on effective teaching, coaching relationships for both teachers and administrators, and a significant dependence on the expertise of consultants. Finally, schools that passed successfully through this second stage apparently became more independent in their ability to constructively manage their improvement. Like Elmore's work, Gray's model of improvement in low-performing schools is theoretical; the schools that he studied were highly variable in both their context, their specific responses to external accountability, the pace of their improvement, and their overall outcomes. Still, the value of these two descriptions to an understanding of improvement in low-performing schools is critical: there is just no simple way around the tough problems related to improvement and the development of internal capacity, and the solution to these problems requires more than what a low-performing school's existing capacities can provide.

Second Complication: Different Levels of Internal Accountability

Also critical to the variation in low-performing schools prior to state intervention is internal capacity. In this formulation, internal accountability is a precondition to a school's effective response to the demands of an external accountability system, and schools are not improved only because they are subject to the intervention of the state even if the stakes of such a system are perceived by teachers to be high.[13] Rather, state accountability "sets in motion a complex chain of events that may ultimately improve teaching and learning."[14] This complex chain, and each of the variables in it, is daunting. It is made up of the unique cultural, historical, organizational, and professional characteristics of each school, and no two schools are the same in the specifics of their internal accountability. For example, a school's internal accountability will vary in how much the school views subject-area expertise as an excuse for overspecialization and isolation. Other aspects of internal accountability include the organization's particular definition of leadership as either individual or distributed and the school's access to, and use of, critical resources such as time, information about effective instruction, and money.

Schools also differ in how teachers address students' learning challenges and in the schools' relationship between the goals of the state's accountability policies and the school's mission.[15] There are also meaningful distinctions in how much variation in instructional practice and student outcomes schools will accept and in the relationship between schools' administrative practices and improved teaching and learning. Moreover, teachers differ in how—or whether—they can conceive of change in their schools and can enact it. This capacity for change is related to the particular experiences of a school staff with policy, leadership, the allocation of resources, and their past impact on the establishment of goals.[16]

As a quick gauge of internal accountability, if teachers possess a strong ethic of investigation and collaboration about the stickiest aspects of their practice and have a history of success with these things, they are likely to respond to external accountability in the way that policy makers imagine. Despite these assurances, however, an individual school's adaptive response to state policy is anything but guaranteed.

The implications of these assertions are profound for low-performing schools and the systems designed to improve them. First, the interaction of a complex set of variables (including structures for professional learning and leadership, both of which are discussed in the coming sections) that exist prior to the arrival of any accountability measures most determines a school's reaction. Second, state accountability does not create the conditions for internal accountability; in fact, accountability systems and their public pressures may encourage schools to behave in ways that inhibit the development of internal capacity. Third, because internal accountability supposes an attention to improving the quality of teaching and learning—historically the least-examined aspect of schools' work—improvement is difficult, time-consuming, and often beyond the skills and knowledge of the people working in low-performing schools.[17]

Third Complication: Variable Quality and Skill of School Leaders

Time and again, research on low-performing schools points to the centrality of school principals to any effort to satisfy the relatively high performance demands of state accountability systems. To say that principals are at the center of this current round of school reform is to understate the case: they are so far the only school employees to have been removed from their positions as a result of poor student performance, and more than any other person in schools, they set the tone for their school's response. If a school succeeds, principals are widely given the credit; if the school continues to founder, principals find themselves on the proverbial block.

Various studies have looked at the skills required of principals in low-performing schools and are relevant to a discussion of schools' reactions to state accountability. There is little point in creating a catalog of these skills; principals must know how and when, and with which constituency, to utilize a broad range of skills, and there is no single formula for employing these skills.[18] Instead, principals must possess a theory, articulate it in sufficient detail and with enough political acumen to engage an effective group within the school, and be committed to ongoing revision. This is what researchers have described as a "ready, fire, aim" approach: the problems faced by low-performing schools are sufficiently complex that there is neither a master plan that can be exported from outside the school, nor an internal plan capable of responding to what an intentional school will learn in the course of trying to get better.[19]

Other authorities have similarly concluded that a principal's work is so expansive that they prefer to describe these skills categorically. In the main, principals must possess skills in four complementary realms: instructional leadership, distributed leadership, transformative leadership, and results-driven leadership.[20] Though the core task is the systematic improvement of instruction for all teachers and of learning for all students, the paths to this goal are many—and each must be navigated at the same time. It's essential that principals know good instruction: they must recognize it, in each subject area, and be able to analyze patterns in any teachers' practice. They must also focus on aligning curricula, create structures for teachers to meet, and ensure that these meetings are of sufficient quality to build a sense of mutual responsibility and inclusion among teachers.[21] Principals need to identify, manage, and make sense of multiple sources of meaningful and timely data. And they must work outside the school, too, engaging in partnerships that bring resources.[22] The job, in all its many facets, is to provide stability—and, in equal measures, to press for change.[23]

In effect, all the principal's traditional tasks—particularly the political and managerial—remain.[24] The new work of managing instructional improvement—in the face of a static set of rules about the workplace and the increasing pressures of test-based accountability—now defines the effective principal.

Without a doubt, being a principal now is more complicated than ever before. The position is nevertheless still bound by all the same constraints that existed in any other era of reform. Principals still face the same challenges with respect to their control of time; other resources such as money, program flexibility, and support; and the local politics of public education.[25] Principals are meant to perform nearly every task outside of classroom teaching, and they are immensely disadvantaged by a uniquely American perspective on leadership: they are assumed to aspire to, and be capable of filling, a hero's role.[26] Add to this the new challenges that principals report with the advent of test-based, high-stakes accountability, and the mix is indeed formidable. These new challenges include testing systems that may not support high-quality teaching; the perverse incentives that may lead to a narrowing of the curriculum and a misuse of instructional time; the need to attend to every subgroup in the school; and dramatically heightened levels of anxiety among teachers, parents, and students.[27] Many principals must contend with these additional aspects of the low-performing school, and they bring with them no new form of support. These challenges add to the complexity of the work and represent additional ways in which a solid improvement trajectory, now an imperative under high-stakes accountability, might be derailed.

Fourth Complication: Differences in School Districts

Another aspect of the differences among low-performing schools pertains to the state and district contexts in which these schools reside—and from whose cues, structures, and direction low-performing schools craft their responses to external accountability. In general, policy makers assume that state accountability systems will improve the motivation of the professionals in these school and will thereby squeeze out the results that had previously eluded the schools.[28]

In reality, though, states have few resources for their struggling schools, which contend with large differences in the intensity and type of state support. States have created their own systems that vary with respect to how and when school leaders are replaced; the number of years allowed for improving student achievement; and the inclusion of social- and school-climate-related goals in school improvement plans.[29] States have also come up with different explanations of their system's rationale and have placed different levels of emphasis on professional development, coaches, and professional learning teams.[30]

In the wake of this uneven policy landscape, researchers have pointed out that local districts—where relatively little attention has been paid by lawmakers so far—exert a good deal of influence on low-performing schools' improvement efforts.[31] They point to the importance of numerous district-level variables in the success of low-performing schools. These local variables can range from the operational to the cultural: district policies on student enrollment, transportation, and teacher recruitment; the extent to which district personnel accept responsibility for low performance; and equity considerations in decisions related to staffing, budgeting, and support.[32] Also important is the districts' awareness of the negative incentives associated with test-based accountability and the amount of cooperation between the union and district administrators prior to state intervention.[33] Local school districts may also play important roles in facilitating partnerships for low-performing schools;

supporting new, substantive instructional leadership; establishing a politically viable vision that helps sustain multiple reform efforts over time; providing useful and timely benchmark data to schools that emphasize higher-order thinking skills; and establishing instructional and curricular coherence.[34] Despite the relevance of school districts to school improvement, many states around the country make no concerted effort either to support local school districts or even to include them in key accountability decisions when requiring the low-performing schools—like the three Massachusetts schools in this study—to respond to state accountability.

Taken together, these findings from low-performing schools say something profound—and damning—about the ways most states have gone about improving education in these institutions. The glaring headline is that the current generation of state accountability and intervention simply doesn't possess the level of nuance or discernment that is needed to affect each school in either the intensity or the manner that it's needed. We've been assuming that the people in low-performing schools are facing a relatively similar set of challenges and that there is a similar course for each to follow. At some basic level, this is true: every school in this position has its hardest work to do in its classrooms, making instructional quality a feature of all its classes. But how it leverages its strengths, accounts for its own history, faces the shortcomings in the skills of its staff, and brings new ideas into the fold—these things, and many more, are matters of strategy. These issues of organizational development are missing in the current formulation of state intervention.

If the differences in low-performing schools are one key reason that intervention isn't working the way it was hoped, is there anything else going on as well? Why are these massive efforts and substantial outlays of time and money producing only a pittance of results?

Foundational Facts of Low-Performing Schools Are Unaffected by State Accountability

A second answer to what's going wrong with intervention has to do with the fixed features of innumerable schools—the things that certainly shaped day-to-day life at Stoddard, Tanner, and Connington. As much as intervention expects that people in these schools will spend their time in different ways and focus on different work, it doesn't work on the basic organizational features of schools. There's still no more time in the day and no fewer students. Teachers' collective bargaining agreements still define key parts of the schools' basic arrangements: which teachers stay in the schools; which teachers may enter and exit, and under what conditions; which teachers are doing well and which are not; and, of much importance, who has the authority to establish common expectations for proficient instructional practice. Even in the most intense stages of intervention, principals and teachers stay deeply isolated from new knowledge of other similarly situated schools—to the extent that this learning exists. Shop politics still carry the day. With the wrecking ball in full swing, it's as if the position of brick after brick in the foundation of these schools remains unaltered. And in the things that stay the same—in all these "foundational facts"—we find the second part of the answer to why intervention is not working.

Fundamentally, Stoddard, Tanner, and Connington Schools were trying to meet new ends through well-worn means. They were using the same professional development, the same meeting time, the same concepts and methods, and even the same language about teaching to try to produce gains in student achievement. At Stoddard, the same relationship between young and veteran teachers continued to exist, and PIM only heightened this tension. At Tanner, principal Trisha Waighn resurrected the same methodology from her days as a reading teacher twenty years ago and then exhorted her teachers to simply try something new. For her, this rehashing was strategic, and she did so for expressly historical reasons: she had come to believe, through hard-fought experience, that her supervision and the evaluation process wouldn't produce the changes she wanted. At Connington, the district still bussed its students across town, pulled advanced students into its special programs, and loaded up underperforming schools with a disproportionate number of classes for English language learners and special education students. Each of these three principals described the acute balancing required of them; by necessity, they had to translate the urgency of state intervention into a local, closed system of fixed rules.

For all schools, the results of these competing pressures are surprising—and fly in the face of what outside intervention is supposed to do. At ground level, the steps that policy makers see as inevitable consequences of state intervention—the data analysis, the planning, and the uptake of new and more powerful ideas—are anything but inevitable. Certainly, this work is taking place in name, but it's conditional. It's filtered through ground-level realities. For principals and anyone else with a bent to lead, it introduces a set of dilemmas with multiple solutions. One can well imagine the trunk of a tree as a metaphor for the data analysis, planning, and new strategies that are the core intervention activities in most states. To see how schools are reacting to these interventions, imagine now a chaotic spread of branches, every one the result of some local calculation to fit the intervention into a school with a finite ability to change without collapsing altogether. The collapse isn't literal; for example, it was the three or more years of roiling dissatisfaction that Connington experienced. This was what the principals at Stoddard and Tanner Schools were taking great pains to avoid. In an organization in which teachers retain dozens of ways to veto any new effort, everything is a dilemma. Everything is political.

So here are the two key, unaltered foundational facts of low-performing schools. They underlie these schools' response to external accountability.

First Foundational Fact: Grave Professional Isolation

At Stoddard, perhaps the most important domain in which PIM team members needed to take action had to do with their ideas about how schools change. In the absence of any training about change theories, team members developed their own particular theories about how to alter teaching and learning, and the processes that the team developed for such critical activities like professional development, walk-throughs, teacher collaboration, and collecting and analyzing data about implementation were all affected by these beliefs. Professional development continued to be a voluntary pursuit at the school; the school continued its relationships with consultants and community organizations with no new regard for the goals laid out in the plan, and the Harborview central office continued to approve in-service offerings provided by teachers to their peers, with only a consideration for the preference of the teacher-providers. Walk-throughs were conceived of as an opportunity to provide moral support and build relationships; administrators continued to stand in hallways, offering polite observations and supervising students. PIM team members made informal polls of the teachers they knew as a measure of how much—and how well—a strategy was being implemented. Though the plan asked for very specific measures and required the identification of every individual responsible for implementing the plan, the actual process was quite different. And in every case, PIM team members talked about their own ideas of how to support change. In this sense, the rigor of PIM wasn't diluted exclusively by a lack of will or time, but by team members' own best intentions—by their own improvised theories of change.

As described in chapter 1, Stoddard's PIM team members relied heavily on issuing memos, calendars, and notes to their colleagues—and that this was their sole means for effecting change at the school. This practice represented a considerable change for the school and most certainly for the young teachers on the team. They were willfully placing themselves in a different position with respect to their peers; in fact, in the seniority-based culture of the school, all the team members felt strongly that they had severely overstepped Stoddard's unspoken limits. The point here is not the risk, however. It's that issuing memos represented the least offensive means of action available to the team. Memos were the least they could do, and the team used the written word because to employ other, more direct means of communication not only violated the politics of the place, but wasn't really necessary, in their opinion. Teachers at Stoddard basically knew how to do what the PIM team was asking them to. Given the proper level of goodwill and the right adjustments to teachers' motivations, the teaching strategies identified by the PIM team would begin to appear in most of the school's classrooms.

From principal to teacher-leaders, this is what Stoddard was banking on, and it was not at all unlike the story coming from Tanner School. In both places, school leaders were left by the state and district to develop their own theory of change, and the schools believed that improvement would be mostly a function of teachers' attitudes toward practices they could just choose to deliver—if only they could be persuaded.

The unsettling consequence of these improvised theories was how thoroughly it left out the professional development needs of teachers in these two schools. It was also a setup for even greater levels of tension between each school's "reformers" and "resistors." If everyone already knows how to improve student learning but is choosing not to, then there's little explanation left except that those who are not improving are simply resistant. It's an obvious reinforcement of an old us-versus-them idea, one that's had plenty of play in American schools. The idea is also contrary to the great need for real gains in low-performing schools. Where the intervention supposes a higher-quality discourse in target schools than truly exists, then old, worn-out ideas become more entrenched in these schools. Of the three schools detailed in this book, two succumbed to this dynamic. In effect, they didn't really get out of the gate. It's not that Stoddard and Tanner schools ultimately failed; it's that the fundamentals of the state's reforms strategies—the local use of assessment data, the planning, and the targeted professional learning—didn't even enter the bloodstream. If these three schools are numerically representative of low-performing schools, then the early failure of two of them represents a massive proportion with intervention.

Connington's quiet teacher meetings represented a different kind of failure. The principal obviously understood that intervention was about his staff's learning new skills, and he was oriented toward the creation of a professional learning community. But after years of grueling interactions and clearing the ranks of teachers who were unwilling to buy in, he found that he couldn't move his teachers past their fear of him. The school's ethic of teachers' individual autonomy was replaced by a different orthodoxy. This was a new kind of passivity—not so much resistant, as it was in Martinez's early years, as stumped. Teachers were consistently complying with his expectations, but as a group, they were not any more able to examine the results of their work, ask critical questions, and adapt. Understandably, there was also a sense of comfort at Connington. This was a comfort borne not of any greatly improved outcomes for students, but from the staff's having taken all the steps that were asked of them. They did the work required of them as part of intervention. The new curriculum was there; the data systems were active; the tiered intervention programs for struggling students were in place; the well-planned meetings took place regularly. Though Connington was still among the lowest-performing schools in the state, the school's educators took some cold comfort in having finished the plan.

Whatever the core reason for each school's foundering—whether it was one school's hope that imploring would work, or another's lopsided use of control—all of this was ultimately commentary on the profound isolation of each of these schools. Despite intervention, all three schools were left on their own to answer decisive questions about what needed to improve and how this would be accomplished. They had to invent their own theories of change. Their answers to these questions would profoundly shape everything that followed. At Stoddard, this led to essentially a strategy that went heavy on written appeals for change, with little attention to professional learning and no mechanism for inspecting the classroom. At Tanner, teachers were only too happy to allow Trisha Waighn, their principal, to establish the superintendent's after-school programs; meanwhile, they rejected her legitimacy in all matters related to the way they taught during the school day. At Connington, the initial near impossibility of focusing on professional learning led to confrontation, control, and a durable period of fear. This last school got the farthest, but only with respect to the ancillary components of intervention; it never raised students' achievement in an adequate way.

Connington holds another lesson about isolation—a lesson explained well by Jessica Hereford, an insightful Connington teacher. Hereford said that the school's improvement strategy was based on little more than good luck, or what she termed serendipity. Fine, she seemed to be saying, the school was better staffed and better organized. Everyone did what was asked of them as part of the state's intervention. The teachers were motivated to do right by the students they taught. And, even with all this, the staff was only just hoping for the next good idea—whatever it was—to come from somewhere: an especially productive team meeting, a Connington classroom, the district, an article, a consultant. If the test scores required that the school continue to adjust and improve, then how should this be done? What would be a smart next move for a school with its bases covered? Quite clearly, no one at Connington had any idea, and no one from the district or state had anything at all to say on the subject. In year seven of intervention and high on the state's watch list, Connington School was gravely, inexcusably isolated.

Much the same tune played in all the schools. Fundamentally, their varied responses to intervention had one thing in common. They were all improvised. They were conceived alone and enacted alone. Whether it was in the form of the language they used to describe instruction, how they behaved as leaders, or how they conceived of the barriers to student learning, they all made unjustifiably large withdrawals from the same bank of ideas they'd employed in the past. In fact, there was no other reserve from which to draw.

In the ever-devolving relationship between state, district, and school, the final message would have been remarkably simple to follow: form teams, look at your data, write a plan, replace core instructional programs. If this were all it took, then intervention would have been very straightforward.

But if each of these required activities surrenders something vital because of any school's isolation, then what? And what if there is only a one-in-three chance that each piece is created in the way it was supposed to be, but then the pieces don't cohere into an organized and effective whole? Regrettably, the answers are found easily enough in the stories of Stoddard, Tanner, and Connington. Such is the nature of this grave professional isolation, and at this point in the evolution of intervention in low-performing schools, there's not much help on the way.

Second Foundational Fact: Persistent Sources of Instability

In the quiet years before their designation as underperforming schools, all three of the schools in this book enjoyed a good deal of consistency in their teaching faculty. Teachers rarely moved from one district school to another, and large groups of teachers became close-knit. They became personal friends—loyal to one another, drawn inward, and wary of disruptive energy.

At Connington, this was the backdrop to Jesse Martinez's arrival as principal and the precursor to the declarations of the state. Within months, this equilibrium came apart, and the stability started to erode. As he became familiar with the internal workings of his staff, Martinez decided that charging hard into the group's sense of self-satisfaction was the only option open to him. Connington would most certainly have not made any progress, considering its widespread resistance to the notion that teachers were responsible for the educational outcomes of their students. It may have been necessary for Martinez to adopt such hard-nosed tactics, but it would be five full years before the school found its way out of the conflict.

Martinez was willing to pass the limits that had previously held Connington together. He saw no other way forward for his school, and his superiors apparently endorsed his approach. Martinez was willing to rattle the cage; he was willing to put what he wanted in writing, to rove through the school looking for the improvements he wanted, and to challenge the teachers he thought weren't delivering.

Whether these confrontational tactics were necessary or not, one significant problem with them was that by 2007, Connington stuck in a negative feedback loop of teacher turnover. As described in chapter 2, the gains from increased staff participation were offset by the inexperience of newly hired teachers. These new teachers, with few skills to address the problems of an underperforming school, were more likely to leave, thereby necessitating the hiring of new teachers for the next year, when the cycle of overwhelming problems would continue.

The experiences of Connington, Stoddard, and Tanner, fell into a pattern. By asking each school to bring its data into its planning, external intervention was meant to introduce a new dynamic into these schools and to have each school adhere to a new logic. The goal was for each school to understand that to improve learning, teaching also had to be improved.

To achieve this understanding, however, school leaders had to enter into a complicated relationship with the remainder of the staff. Many difficult issues were necessarily raised through these complicated interactions; among the most prominent issues was who had legitimate authority over what the teachers considered the most intimate aspects of their work. Whether framed as a question of contract-based tenure, seniority-based expertise, or some other thing related to evaluation or academic freedom, the issue took center stage in every school. This question about who was in control—at ten o'clock on any given school day, in the middle of a math lesson, or as it related to what teachers and students say and do— was inescapable. And remarkably, as much as the state intended a single, effective response to this question from each of its lowest-performing schools, each school had available to it a range of answers. What's more, nearly everything about each school's response stemmed from its initial resolution of the question of authority. As much as the state intended an inexorable march, it produced only a scattered crawl.

To understand how powerful the question of authority really is, one need only see what happened at Connington in its first years. Martinez resolved this question about authority in a definitive manner. In what he saw as an absence of effective practice among the staff he inherited, he claimed all the authority for himself. And from this initial decision, five years of disruption and acrimony followed. Whether Martinez's authoritarian approach was necessary and in the long-term interest of future Connington students is a matter of debate. In any case, the approach undeniably brought heavy consequences for Martinez and every other adult working at the school. Connington became a miserable and lonely place to work. And this possibility—that work might become so miserable and lonely—was the counterweight to the impulse of intervention and it bore heavily on Tanner's Trisha Waighn and Stoddard's Ken Schumer as they weighed what the state began requiring of them. To be sure, all of the schools had formal rules related to observations, feedback, and evaluation. There were also more muted notions about academic freedom. But for the most part, principals and teacher-leaders filtered out most of the expectations they believed might have crossed a boundary. The limits were mostly unspoken, powerful, and almost fully self-imposed.

In between intervention and the hefty counterweight of their school's potential for unhappy instability, each of these three principals made very different decisions. Martinez bore down and confronted his teachers, paying a personal price for this toil, and eventually remade his staff. Waighn looked to what she could change outside Tanner's classrooms and outside the school day. Schumer put himself in the backseat, deferring to his PIM team teachers, who in turn waged a mostly informal campaign of compliments and memo writing.

Whether it was confronting, deflecting, or deferring, each of these decisions was definitive for the school and simultaneously opened and closed certain options for how the schools could move ahead. Each decision stemmed from what is really the fundamental dilemma of intervention in schools: at the ground level, schools must reconcile the countervailing needs of both improving teaching and maintaining stability. Everything else—every other decision that follows—is fruit from the same tree.

One very important point here is that sanctions and mandates—even for the most common requirements like data analysis, strategic planning, and adopting new materials—are far from impermeable. In fact, they appear to leak pretty quickly. The manner in which each of the three schools in this book resolved the dilemma of instructional improvement versus stability served as a filter to the state's required work. This was how Stoddard's intervention team co-opted PIM so that the process primarily served as a tool for securing the peace; they went to their colleagues intending to create a final plan that would reflect the staff's preexisting teaching preferences. This was how Tanner's teachers could hold accountability at arm's length, leaving their principal to stay at school until six every night to supervise after-school test-preparation programs. And it was how Connington's teachers could personalize the state's expectations for the school.

A Compliance Mind-Set

In addition to the problems of individual school differences and the foundational facts discussed above, there is one last important lesson from the stories of the three schools in this book. This third lesson has to do with how easily each school slipped into a sense of satisfaction about having complied with the requirements of intervention, even if these actions had no discernible effect on student achievement. The teachers and principals in these schools very readily described their sense of accomplishment in having completed the state's planning process or in having submitted the agendas from the meetings required by the district as proof that the meetings had taken place. These steps, and many others like them, appeared to represent for them a terminus of sorts, rather than a way station en route to a larger goal.

Paradoxically, the real way station, the one that researchers identify as an important precursor to sustained growth in student achievement, is not so much the completion of tasks as it is the ability to learn from them in a coherent, all-hands-on-deck fashion. At Stoddard, Tanner, and Connington Schools, there was relatively little evidence of this sort of learning. Rather, plans, meetings, agendas, and even whole instructional programs were ends unto themselves, and as much as these schools deserved to mark their progress in implementing new work, the goal was never only to rearrange the out-of-classroom work of the adults. If the work has no observable impact on the capacity of the staff to deliver instruction of a higher quality, then the work misses its mark. Quite obviously, there is real risk when a school substitutes its improvement activities for real improvements in student learning.

The compliance orientation has more than one risk. Sometimes, compliance can become a kind of raison d'être, supplanting an interest in improved teaching and learning for a begrudging going-along. Take Stoddard School as one manifestation of how compliance can become the cause itself. In this school, compliance with state PIM requirements became the rallying cry of the PIM team. This was the reason they gave their colleagues for all the plan's variety of activities, from additional meetings to teacher surveys to new instructional approaches. This strategy wasn't necessarily bad; in the absence of agreement among teachers that the school even had a problem, this may have been the cover the team needed just to get the ball rolling. But the lack of inclusion in the approach led many Stoddard teachers to simply close their classroom doors, and no one in the school was thinking about what would happen if the required activities didn't actually work. More significant still, by finding an external enemy in the state, the school clearly avoided internalizing its responsibilities. In the school's affinity for compliance, teachers won for themselves the comfort that comes from saying something like See, we're doing what you told us to. What's more, this comfort turned into something like smugness when the PIM plan failed to yield results.

Consider, however, the costs of this comfort. Gone is the capacity to diagnose challenges. Wiped out is the ability solve the problems that inevitably spring from a first round of effort. Compliance is the greatly cheapened version of a school's engagement in intervention, and sadly, there's far greater incentive for teachers to adopt this mind-set than there is to accept ownership. And especially for principals, for whom questions about teachers' professionalism and motivation are the fastest course to mutiny, adopting the framing of compliance just might be the safest choice they have left to make.

Tanner School provides us with a different view of the problem. As described in chapter 2, the more powerful intervention impulse for Tanner—and for the many schools in a similar situation—had to do with the district's performance-improvement status. The school had missed its performance target for a single year, but the district had failed to do so for three. The after-school programs that Principal Waighn was required to launch were part of the district's burden to the state and then became—without any discussion between Waighn and the district— part of the school's burden to the district. At the school, this arrangement gave teachers an unusually easy target for criticism, because no part of the plan was theirs. For this reason, many teachers at the Tanner, when asked about intervention, could shrug their shoulders and issue the breezy encouragement, "I just hope Trish can pull it off." It was an administrative obligation stemming from an administrative problem.

The relationship between Tanner School and its district, Hoover Public Schools, suggested something more troubling than what the offhanded remarks of the teachers indicated. As discussed earlier, research has concluded that districts have a powerful role in improving low-performing schools, and the most effective districts have aimed their support as close to classroom instruction as possible. These few districts have learned to listen to schools and the professional-learning problems the schools face. In Tanner's case, the district—and by extension, the state—had inverted this relationship. The district and its obligations to the state were now client to the schools. The information flow, as much as it had traditionally gone from district to school, anyway, now did so with the imprimatur of the state. And at the very moment that Tanner's teachers needed to engage with their new status as an underperforming school and, ultimately, to locate responsibility and agency within their ranks, the district just told them what to do. For a group used to this arrangement, it felt a lot like another reason to close the classroom door.

In the end, this is a massive failure of discernment, a kind of blindness to the differences between the needs of the district and the more particular needs of the school. As part of its responsibilities in administering No Child Left Behind, the state had every right to ask the district to think about more effective uses of its extended-time programs. But as a uniform district initiative, the after-school programs should never have stripped the focus from Tanner's classrooms. It might have been the fault of the superintendent that this happened, or maybe that of the principal. In any case, this problem was a consequence of the type of two-tiered accountability that is operating in most states right now. If the district is handed one set of obligations as a result of its accountability status, district leaders will look to fulfill these obligations: they will pass the work down to schools for implementation. If schools are given another set of expectations as a result of their own accountability status, some level of conflict will occur, naturally triggering in schools the compliance orientation. If, however, the aim of all this intervention is, as it ought to be, to facilitate schools' own internal accountability as a means of achieving sustained growth, this two-tiered accountability may be not only redundant, but self-defeating as well.

Ultimately, students learn in classrooms, classrooms sit in schools, schools exist within district, and districts make up the state. Effective intervention in struggling schools must not ignore this basic relationship or fail to understand the challenges faced by students, teachers, and their schools. For every step closer to students you seek to intervene, it's another level of discernment required—a willingness to deal with the particulars of individual schools and individual teachers. The stories from Stoddard, Tanner, and Connington suggest that there is no shortcut to this work and that the compliance orientation of teachers, principals, and schools is a risk built into the system. This sort of response—cynical, self-protective, and often deeply historical—can by itself derail any attempt to intervene in a low-performing school. And for some reason, perhaps because it's cultural and psychological and not readily measured or included in a plan, it's something that was ignored in the three schools in this book.

Addressing the Three Common Problems of Intervention

With the advantage of some close inspection, this chapter has laid out what seems to be going awry with our current intervention practices. Despite the overwhelming number of variables in so complicated a system as public schools, three overarching ideas still hold. First, low-performing schools are actually more different—with respect to their development, the level of internal accountability, their leadership, and their district—than anyone has been imagining. Second, intervention has so far made no real alteration to the foundational facts of most schools. It has failed to reduce the grave isolation of these schools or to address their basic sources of instability. Third, intervention has so far ignored that compliance can be its own comfort for low-performing schools and that the compliance orientation alone can dramatically shape their work. These factors combined present a more sober picture of the work that's needed and a clearer explanation of why intervention systems have had such little lasting impact on low-performing schools.

So, here is the question. After more than ten years of all these efforts to fix low-performing schools, and with so little to show for it, what needs to happen now? Is it the current increase in new charters? Is it a run on tenure? Or is it, as an absolutely necessary complement to any new effort, a better form of help? Because a new iteration of intervention is so badly needed, what should the new version look like? What should it include? And what should it discard?

What can be so frustrating about the most recent discoveries about improving low-performing schools isn't so much that these challenges exist. It's that they've been ignored almost completely and that there has been no systemic response to the patterns in schools' struggles. Low-performing schools may be complicated and variable in their particulars, but they wrestle with the same dilemmas. They are subject to the same rules, the same sources of instability, the same limitations on leadership, and generally the same relationships with their districts and states. More than is currently reflected in state intervention design, these shared features are known quantities, and however neglected they've been so far, their effects are predictable. The next generation of intervention design ought to use a more sophisticated knowledge of low-performing schools and how they work, replacing a single theoretical response—something like performance data leading to self-reckoning and improved motivation, which then leads to better teaching and improved learning—with a real account of how these schools respond to external accountability.

For anyone concerned about improving the assistance that low-performing schools receive, there is a silver lining: the next generation of intervention has some clear starting points. The remainder of this book explains and describes three new principles for the reconceptualization of school intervention in this country. First, intervention should begin with the creation of a developmental profile and strategy for each school. Second, intervention should be considered a staged implementation, with a set of defined, incremental steps designed to move schools more efficiently from basic problems of organization to the more complex problems of organizational learning. Third, intervention should set the stage for serious collaborative learning and problem solving, primarily as this concerns the many slow, bloated ways in which so many low-performing districts conduct their business. These principles for schools, districts, states, and third-party providers of support are about policy and practice and will require, if put into place, some very deliberate recasting of the operating conditions of low-performing schools.

5

Creating a Developmental Profile to Assess Schools' Needs

I n light of the quick snapshot of the systemic dysfunction presented in the preceding chapters, the next generation of intervention in low-performing schools must address certain issues more effectively: first, when low-performing schools begin to interact with the state accountability system, they are already laden with cultural and political impediments to most efforts at collective improvement. For the majority of schools, where there is no maverick superintendent or political iconoclast, this situation is just not going to change. Accordingly, these cultural and political impediments naturally create dilemmas for school leaders, and how these leaders resolve these dilemmas—day after day, year after year—greatly affects their schools' ability to form strong internal accountability. In the absence of a pedagogical and organizational expertise—that is, if nothing is done to break the long history of isolation in most low-performing schools—schools are not likely to resolve these dilemmas in ways that *efficiently* heighten their internal accountability. Without the support, mutual expectations, and commitment to coherent change that are the hallmarks of schools with high levels of internal accountability, teachers' capacity to create more powerful learning experiences in every class in the school remains equally low, as do the test scores their students earn. While aggregate scores may bump up here and there, schools locked in this pattern make only intermittent and marginal gains.

For many intervention schools, this sequence of mostly low performance with an occasional bump has been going on for quite some time. The key, then, is to find new, more effective ways for low-performing schools to experience sustained growth more often. The remainder of this book is devoted to this task.

As we move forward, it's important to keep in mind the three central reasons, described in chapter 4, that the current round of accountability isn't doing what we'd hoped. First, low-performing schools are generally much more complicated entities than state accountability systems have allowed. Most significantly, they vary in the pace of their improvement, in the degree to which they hold themselves collectively accountable for their results, in the quality of the leadership, and in the level of support they receive from their district. Second, state accountability doesn't reset any of the foundational facts that shape the operation of low-performing schools. Most importantly, intervention so far does little to counter the isolation faced by these schools or to reset—or at least account for—their sources of instability. Third, intervention leaves unexamined the powerful allure, and powerful drag, of the compliance-oriented response. These three findings are the mortar for a new kind of construction, and notably, the struggles of the schools in this book are the consequences of leaving these problems unattended.

If there is a single variable missing from current intervention systems, it's the effort to nurture a *developmental strategy* within each school. Indeed, there's no attention at all to the organizational development that might reasonably occur over time for most schools. A far smarter strategy for a low-performing school would consistently guide a principal and teacher-leaders to understand their school in terms of the general pattern of growth for similar schools, and then provide ongoing support so that the educators could make more informed decisions about which improvement activities are most likely to move the school from one developmental stage to the next. Improvements in student learning are certainly the goal, but our most recent understanding is that these improvements tend to be temporary and marginal if schools are not pursuing a course toward demanding and skilled teaching. This level of teaching generally is most frequently achieved in schools with high internal accountability: where teachers trust one another, establish mutual expectations for their teaching, and are able to learn out in the open. These are the components of an effective school culture, and low-performing schools must be supported to move stepwise toward this goal. The alternative to paying attention to helping schools establish their own developmental strategy is many more years of the hunt-and-peck work that the current system produces in such abundance.

To take on the shortcomings of our current system of school intervention—the inattention both to schools' variability and to the effects of their isolation, culture, and politics—the next generation of intervention must finely differentiate low-performing schools. Intervention will need an approach that is both developmental and organizational—neither of which figures much into the way that states are compelled by NCLB to count only the number of years that a school hasn't met its performance targets. Moreover, an enriched intervention system will need to act on schools' isolation, both by encouraging school and district leaders to understand the general patterns of improvement in low-performing schools and then by rallying them around a developmental strategy for each school. This means that policy makers and support providers, whether they work at the state or district level, must learn to embrace the particulars of the low-performing schools they hope to help improve.

As these things start to happen, the next generation of intervention will also need to set the stage for high-level instruction and collaborative problem solving—two capabilities in increasingly short supply in low-performing schools. Too often, low-performing schools like Stoddard and Tanner spend years in pursuit of relatively low-level changes to students' learning experiences, looking to remedial camps and test preparation programs as a facile sort of balm. To prevent this all-too-common outcome, a more thoughtful intervention system must lay the foundation for substantive improvements in a school's curriculum, instruction, and assessment. That is, districts and schools must prepare for the truly challenging work of classroom-by-classroom improvements to teaching, an endeavor that is resource intensive, specific, and fundamentally about professional learning. Nothing about current intervention consistently assures that this work is taken up.

The idea that intervention must become developmental represents several significant changes from the status quo and should be the conceptual cornerstones of the next generation of school intervention.

Determining a School's Developmental Stage

Addressing the need for a developmental strategy means that schools, districts, and state support providers must work together to assess each school's place along a developmental continuum. Filling in the gap in current intervention design means that states and districts—inasmuch as they seek to help schools and not simply hold them accountable—should pay attention to more than just test scores. Additional measures should include an expanded understanding of student learning, school culture, teachers' views about trust, and how and if the school's structure supports professional learning. This assessment mines what we already know about how some low-performing schools have improved. From the cases in this book, for example, we know that schools face the continual resolution of certain key dilemmas, chief among them how to strike a balance between change and stability. School and district leaders' ability to describe these dilemmas provides an important guide for assessing schools.

We also know from the work of Richard Elmore, Heinrich Mintrop, and John Gray that there are at least four critical stages through which low-performing schools pass. This information is critical in comprehending the relative starting position of each school targeted for intervention. We can also derive important assessment information about low-performing schools from the two central bodies of expertise—one pedagogical and the other organizational—that schools must have to increase their internal accountability. Though some of this work is theoretical and there is relatively little research done to map these developmental stages, the concept is solid, important, and robust enough to begin. Given that the variability and isolation of low-performing schools have received little attention despite being so detrimental to these schools, the creation of a new information system for a more nuanced intervention is absolutely critical.

As mentioned before, Stoddard, Tanner, and Connington shared a common set of dilemmas, but were unlike in almost every other way. This alone begged for state accountability systems far more sophisticated in their ability to recognize and respond to important differences in low-performing schools.

Intervention systems should begin with a school profile, developed with a variety of measures that might include the basic disposition of the faculty toward the school's accountability crisis; the school's history of implementing new programs; its ability to produce, manage, and use many kinds of data; its attention to the quality of instruction; the organization and distribution of teacher leadership; and the district's capacity to support change. Such a profile might also consider the relative force of each of the central developmental dilemmas that appeared so prevalent for the schools in this study. The information for this profile shouldn't be viewed as leading to a small set of predetermined paths for improvement, but instead as the basis of some collective strategizing among school leaders, district administrators, and state officials about how to begin the work of improvement. Critically, this step should help local leaders develop a coherent plan for managing the central developmental dilemmas of low-performing schools.

In essence, principals need to be supported to think strategically. They need to ask questions that consider the school's own specific circumstances: Given the morale of the school's teachers, should we pursue improvements that are likely to maintain staff stability, or is a tack that will probably produce unrest and turnover warranted? Given the school's developmental stage, should we focus on creating remedial programs as a step toward improving classroom instruction? What structures for distributed leadership can we create now, despite our teachers' present limited capacity to talk with each other about changes that will apply to every classroom in the school? These questions suggest that every school should possess a plan for building capacity and internal accountability, but this plan must account for local variation. The task is sufficiently complicated that no principal should be in the position of thinking it up on his or her own.

Developmental Profiles for Intervention Schools

To improve low-performing schools more effectively and efficiently, intervention support must prepare a better, specific developmental profile of each of its target schools. This is a radically different approach from the one exercised so much in the last decade, where data, planning, and monitoring were assumed to set every school on a sure trajectory toward improvement. To be discerning, strategic, and smarter, new designs in intervention should create profiles that address the specific struggles of low-performing schools. The steps for looking at these struggles are outlined in the next sections.

Developmental Profile Measure One: How is the school oriented toward the key developmental dilemmas it will face?

The introduction of this book gave a preview of four developmental dilemmas that would repeatedly appear in the stories of the Stoddard, Tanner, and Connington schools. These four dilemmas all centered on the need to balance the forces of change and stability, forces that appear to become even more powerful after state intervention. For principals and teacher-leaders in these three schools, the dilemmas were almost everything. The educators' responses to data, identification of improvement strategies, monitoring of classroom instruction—all these critical components of state intervention were heavily mediated by each school's orientation toward these four developmental dilemmas. In fact, it was each school's earnest attempt to manage these dilemmas that most dramatically led to the idiosyncrasies of their responses to intervention. At each school, the struggle to manage the same basic set of dilemmas came to feel fairly predictable. And for any state intervention system that doesn't consider these dilemmas, the system comes to feel pretty dysfunctional.

A meaningful developmental profile will evaluate each school's response to the key dilemmas the school must address to realize enjoy sustained improvement. Though all the dilemmas relate to the tug between change and stability, there is real value in parsing this tension further, in understanding more specifically what the schools finds most vexing.

So, as you read ahead, keep in mind how powerfully the technical work of intervention—the data analysis, planning, and monitoring—was affected both by the schools' sense of the dilemmas they faced and by how they acted to resolve these problems. For example, data analysis at Stoddard wasn't just about looking at the school's numbers; it was about maintaining the implicit social arrangements between a diverse group of teachers. Classroom visits at Tanner weren't about collecting data and providing feedback, because everyone, including the principal, saw them as incursions into territory that teachers strongly felt was private. In each of these decisions—and there were dozens of critical decisions at each school, stretching over years—there was an active attempt to balance competing interests, to reconcile contrary concerns. The point is that improvement in the low-performing schools is not just a technical process, and nothing about the technical nature of state accountability and intervention reduces this point for the people who work in these schools. Instead, attempts at improvement are also efforts to resolve a set of critical dilemmas about the development of a complex organization.

As these examples show, how a low-performing school is oriented toward the developmental dilemmas and how schools might be tempted, however earnestly, to dilute the intent of intervention are critical questions for the people who seek to support these schools.

DEVELOPMENTAL DILEMMA ONE: THE ATTRIBUTION OF CAUSE

In all three schools discussed in this book, staff members and principals grappled heavily with the source of the problems highlighted in their school's performance data. For the teachers at Stoddard School, low performance was about the decimation of the city's industrial base, the slow slide of civility among their students, and disengaged families and their rough-and-tumble kids. The hallways were a mess, the staff said, because the tumult came from home. Students were impolite, disaffected, and barely engaged because they had been raised this way. These are all reasons external to the school, and at Stoddard—just like Tanner and Connington and so many other schools—it just wasn't a reflection on the teachers. In the view of all these teachers during the earliest stages of intervention—and even again as the promised gains in student achievement never materialized—the internal workings of the school weren't much a part of the conversation either in the teachers' lounge or in the leadership team meetings.

This external-internal dynamic will be familiar to anyone who spends much time in schools. After all, it's far easier to strike up a conversation with a teacher about the infelicities of our popular culture than it is to inquire about the effect of a particular teaching strategy. Even if this dynamic is familiar, it's no less powerful, and intervention design cannot afford to ignore it. This is a key developmental dilemma, and the manner in which a school describes the source of its poor performance is a telling indicator of its location on the trajectory toward internal accountability. (In fact, in most schools, there is probably no single description of the source of poor performance; it usually varies from one camp of teachers in the same school to the next.) Because this dilemma is so powerful for teachers—causing so many teachers to feel blamed, then burned, and ultimately hostile to all external help—the attribution of cause is the first place to begin in assessing the internal workings of a school targeted for intervention.

As a starting point for creating a developmental profile for a low-performing school, then, support providers should consider how responsibility is defined by the educators and administrators they hope to help. Intervention design should include the answers to a few important questions. For example, how do teachers, as a group and as individuals, describe what's going on with the school's poor performance? Is this description internal or external, or some combination of both? Is there consensus or variability among teachers? And what is the relative level of offense among teachers who feel impugned by their school's accountability label?

Beyond these questions, it's important that school leaders and their support providers have some common working understanding about the dynamics that spring up from these divisions. In what proportion can the staff be characterized as either resisting or supporting change? Is this resistance or support passive or vocal?

The importance of these questions is not to find teachers who don't see the value of getting help or who even view themselves as key to the success of their students. Every low-performing school probably has a few teachers who feel this way. What's important is that the school leaders have regular opportunities to work with support providers who are clearly understand this dynamic and who can help the leaders strategically and efficiently improve the faculty's overall sense of responsibility and efficacy.

So, to gain explicit information about attribution as part of a developmental approach to intervention, consider these questions. Would it have been to the advantage of Connington, where teachers barricaded themselves against all forms of instructional improvement, if its early arguments about what caused its failures proceeded in a less alienating or less offensive way? Considering the bloody rows that can spring from the question of who's to blame, was there, in contrast, some advantage to Trisha Waighn's approach at the Tanner? Was her focus on improvements to extended-time interventions a reasonable short-term accommodation to the attitudes of her staff? Better put, consider the more confrontational approach at Connington School: was Jesse Martinez's combative approach on the question of attribution really worth it, especially when the same view seems to reappear among his own hires when the scores never seem to improve enough? Finally, if schools in the first stages of intervention seem likely to go for the low-hanging fruit, anyway, creating remedial and test-prep programs during and after the school day, isn't there probably some time to work on shifting this thinking? As low-performing schools enter the crisis caused by external accountability, perhaps it's a better strategy to only gently prod on the question of attribution than it is to assail it outright. Whatever the best option, intervention design can either take up this question, collecting useful information about how a school is oriented toward this powerful dilemma, or it can leave schools to do so on their own. Given that some schools spend years never moving beyond this bitter stage, here is an excellent place for intervention design to add value.

DEVELOPMENTAL DILEMMA TWO: THE CONTROL OF INSTRUCTION

The second critical developmental dilemma for low-performing schools centers on instructional leadership and the degree to which school leaders, or leadership teams, assume central control of curriculum, instruction, and assessment. The stories in this book show a wide variety of stances toward this kind of control, from Connington School's principal's scripting the agenda for every meeting and taking to the hallways with a teaching checklist of his own design, to Tanner's simple encouragement to avoid the "same old, same old." Out in the larger world of intervention schools, these two examples probably don't even represent the extremes. Control of the instructional process—whether in the form of curriculum, instruction, or assessment—is a hot-button issue just as likely to elicit strong reactions from teachers as is the question of who's to blame for low performance.

Like the attribution of cause, however, the dilemma about control over instruction hasn't yet figured into intervention design. It also has the potential to derail local efforts at improvement and can cost schools years in unnecessary and damaging infighting. Again, this is a question of efficiency. Can the intervention strategy for a particular school be nuanced enough to provide meaningful support for school-based leaders so that they manage this dilemma well—so that the school's path toward internal accountability and sustained growth is as unimpeded as possible? We're not talking about finding a permanent fix so much as making the best match between the need for classroom-by-classroom improvement and the receptivity and capacities of a school's many teachers. And again, either the match is considered explicitly, as a matter of developmental strategy, or it's ignored and left to the skills and inclinations of these long-isolated schools.

What questions should support providers ask to assemble a useful developmental profile related to the dilemma of instructional control? First, they should know where a low-performing school has been, what its history of distributed leadership has been, and what questions about instruction it has considered. Has it taken on any substantive issues related to teaching and learning? Has it mostly followed the lead of its district? Has its attention been close to the classroom and what teachers do during the instructional day, or has it been focused on remediation, after-school programs, or other extracurricular activities?

On a related tack, it's also important for support providers to learn about the extent of instructional expertise at the school. What are the principal's capacities for leading instructional change? How are teachers situated in this regard? And district staff?

In effect, collecting information about this key developmental dilemma means asking some questions—probably no more than good teachers ask about their class at the beginning of a school year, and probably about no larger a group of people than an average class of students. Whether conceived of as qualitative or quantitative work—as a set of regular interviews between school staff and intervention workers or a periodic survey—this information counts. It's important because school leaders need explicit support to understand the opportunities and pitfalls of this dilemma and how it can be managed in support of incrementally more distributed leadership.

DEVELOPMENTAL DILEMMA THREE: THE LOCATION
OF THE RESPONSE TO INTERVENTION

Shot through the stories of the three schools in this book were similar fights about where and how to respond to state intervention requirements.

In this regard, the where and how refer to how close the schools' improvement activities got to teachers' classrooms, and how vigorously the schools insisted on uniform, high-quality implementation. The tug in all the schools, quite obviously, was toward efforts outside the classroom, either in the hallways, on the playground, or after school. These were areas of relative comfort for the schools, and incursions by the principal or leadership team into the territory of individual teachers were usually greeted with some form of pushing back. At Connington, where the incursions were the deepest, the pushing back was forceful, often organized through the teachers union, and lasting. At Tanner, focused as it was on after-school programs, the response was more muted, though every bit as reciprocal: as long as the principal's visits were social, the dissension by teachers remained light.

Connington and Tanner serve as useful counterpoints for describing this dilemma. These aren't new dynamics, however; they're just made more pronounced and urgent by intervention. They're also not exclusive to the schools in this book. This well-described dilemma can be heard in the ongoing concerns among teachers about academic freedom or their complaints about unscheduled observations and evaluation by principals. From the perspective of change agents, this is about the unjustifiable privacy of classroom practice; from the perspective of many teachers, including those who work in low-performing schools, this is about autonomy, professional discretion, and protecting the hard-won right to do right by kids.

Intervention design shouldn't skirt this issue, either, even if it has so far. The dilemma is too real and too powerful for the leaders in low-performing schools to simply ignore it. But these leaders are just too isolated to manage this dilemma, day after day, to move the school as efficiently as possible toward shared, high-quality practice.

As they assemble a developmental profile of each school they hope to help, intervention support providers should also ask question related to where and how schools are striving to make improvements. First, what efforts is the school making so far? Are these efforts related to change in the classroom and to improvements in curriculum, instruction, and assessment? Or are these efforts more concentrated on schoolwide features like extracurricular programs or school climate? If the school is attempting to improve classroom processes, how much of this effort relates to instruction, which is the most private, most skill-based of the three areas listed above?

In addition, it's worth learning what mechanisms the school uses for understanding the extent and quality of its implementation. Is it annual test scores or more frequent formative assessment data? To what other forms of data does the school have access and pay active attention? Does it make use of walk-throughs by either the principal or the teachers, and can it use the results of these inspections? Fundamentally, can the leaders of the school say with any accuracy how many teachers are implementing its classroom initiatives, how well these initiatives are being enacted, and, more challenging yet, how this implementation is affecting student learning?

Of course, this is a lot of information to track and probably more than any support provider, charged with working in many schools at the same time, can use in a meaningful way. The advantage of asking these questions, however, doesn't accrue only to the external help, just as good assessment doesn't only inform the perceptive classroom teacher. By asking these questions—and helping school leaders realize the dilemmas involved in the answers—support providers give the leaders a glimpse into the working of their own school. These questions frame a larger set of possibilities, in the same way that pulling back to a full map gives context to a magnified location. To ask whether a school knows how many teachers are implementing an instructional initiative, and how well they are doing so, is not just a powerful suggestion about what can and should happen. It's the beginning of a conversation, which so far has been absent in intervention design, about how best to get there.

DEVELOPMENTAL DILEMMA FOUR: THE DEFINITION OF THE CHALLENGE

The last of the four dilemmas for the schools in this book centered on defining the challenge facing the school. Fundamentally, the tension that schools experienced in defining the challenge lay between two poles. On one pole, the challenge was viewed as one of compliance with state requirements; on the other, the task was defined as a matter of professional learning.

At one end of this continuum, teachers and principals talked openly about the need to follow the guidelines of the state, even if they disagreed with them. This was the byline of the Stoddard performance improvement mapping team. There's no point in resisting, they said repeatedly to their colleagues, so let's just get the work over with. On the other end of the continuum, teachers and principals spoke about their own need to learn new skills to support students to achieve. There were bits of this at Connington, after five years of purging the old staff, but nothing as robust as it needed to be. Here, on the professional-learning end of the continuum, is where research has shown that schools have the best shot at sustained growth. This is internal accountability, when teachers themselves adopt the disposition of learners and then hold their colleagues to increasingly rich levels of practice and inquiry.

Clearly, most low-performing schools are not self-actualized learning machines. They are somewhere between the self-defeating, self-comforting stance of the compliance orientation and some form of organized professional learning. Where they are on this continuum matters, though, just as it matters that everyone involved in supporting the school has explicit knowledge that this continuum exists. If the goal is to guide schools toward internal accountability and to avoid the traps of the compliance-oriented response, doesn't it make sense that these two things have names?

So, the final element of a developmental assessment for low-performing schools centers on how a school manages the dilemma of compliance versus professional learning. The tendency in this case is clearly toward compliance; this is where the comfort lies. It's important to have a conversation about the principal's own orientation toward this dilemma. It's also important to know how teachers talk about this, and district office staff as well. How do central office demands reinforce the compliance orientation? How is the region's union oriented to this question?

Here is the takeaway of all this talk about developmental dilemmas. The first stage in assessing the developmental needs of low-performing schools is to roughly gauge where a school lies on four important continua. Each of these continua describes a powerful dilemma that most low-performing schools can be expected to face and that, alone or in combination, very often creates significant drag against forward motion. None of these dilemmas is easily resolved or managed, and most schools face them without the advantage of either having them made explicit or any ongoing guidance. This is the core of a system in which positive results, even on paper, appear to be wildly improbable. Out in the real world, you can see the slow progress we're making.

Figure 5.1 shows what the continua of responses to these four developmental dilemmas might look like. One can imagine a team of teachers, a principal, some district office staff, instructional coaches, and third-party support staff working hard to decide where on each of these continua a school belongs. The point of this work isn't judgment; it's that these real forces inside low-performing schools can no longer be ignored.

Keep in mind that the gravitational pull with each of these dilemmas is decidedly toward the left—toward comfort, toward simplicity, toward

Figure 5.1   Continua of Responses to Four Developmental Dilemmas

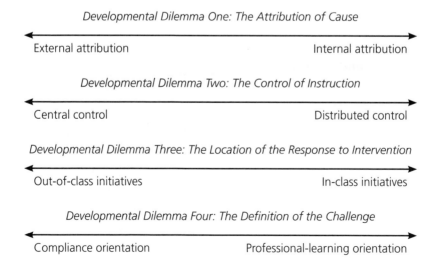

Developmental Dilemma One: The Attribution of Cause

External attribution   Internal attribution

Developmental Dilemma Two: The Control of Instruction

Central control   Distributed control

Developmental Dilemma Three: The Location of the Response to Intervention

Out-of-class initiatives   In-class initiatives

Developmental Dilemma Four: The Definition of the Challenge

Compliance orientation   Professional-learning orientation privacy, and away from conflict. For the principals in this book, the tug toward comfort and privacy was only sometimes explicit. More often, it was something that they felt compellingly. It was longtime experience with the way things are in schools, with what teachers like and don't like. Because most schools don't implode in the way Connington did, these are, by and large, self-reinforcing rules.

There's another benefit to assessing individual schools in terms of their orientation toward these dilemmas, in addition to the value of giving names to the real problems schools face. The assessment creates a frame—maybe any frame—for bridging the gap between low-performing schools and the central office apparatus that is, in theory, supposed to provide support. Today, districts get no help in trying to view their schools in a developmental way. There's nothing to insist that this happen. By considering the predictable dilemmas of schools, this work repositions both district and school; the conversation can pull both toward mutual understanding and support, instead of the more familiar relationship of central office dictates and deep cynicism down in the trenches. When both school and district participate in developing an honest portrait of each school, there's the chance for forming a joint understanding of the challenges and potential in each school. This starting point for the meaningful differentiation of support is what many low-performing schools urgently need.

Developmental Profile, Measure Two: How do the features of the target school relate to the known developmental stages of improving schools?

The second telling measure of a school's developmental profile—and one that should inform the creation of its executive strategy—relates to the general stages of a school's progress. To date, there is still relatively little written about these stages, though the work of Heinrich Mintrop, Richard Elmore, and John Gray provides a rich starting point. The Stoddard, Tanner, and Connington schools, with so many patterns to their common struggles, provide additional guidance. And finally, informative new work about high-poverty, high-performing schools has recently emerged, mainly from the American Enterprise Institute and Mass Insight. (This work is concerned primarily with mapping the features of these inspiring schools and not so much about how low-performing schools move from their current state to one of sustained growth and ongoing success.)

Here, then, are five developmental stages and their key features. Again, schools don't pass on their own from one stage to the next in stepwise fashion, always in advance; a single school can possess features of several stages at once. The central idea here is that these stages exist, that they have describable characteristics, and that intervention policy should be explicit in its intent to coach schools—through tough dilemmas, crises, and moments of great uncertainty—from one stage to the next as efficiently as possible. These stages should be thought of flexibly, and primarily as a means of guidance as schools begin to ask, "Where are we now in our development, and what impact might the decisions we make now have on our ability to develop ourselves?"

STAGE ONE: EMOTIONAL REACTIONS AND QUESTIONS ABOUT
RESPONSIBILITY

Very clearly, we know the most about what happens in schools when they first experience their state's accountability system and learn, usually with great shock and consternation, that they have not met their performance targets. This period is defined by disbelief and other emotions and real questions about the legitimacy of either the measure by which the school is judged or the sanctions it must face. Teachers feel their integrity and professionalism maligned during this period, and they raise questions about the source of poor achievement, often assigning responsibility squarely on families, poverty, the district, and other factors outside the school's control. Not a single school portrayed in this book had an easy time during this stage; in fact, Connington remained in this stage, through massive turnover and deep acrimony, for more than three years.

To judge from the experiences of the three schools in this book, the successful navigation of this stage requires that teachers feel that their concerns about student conduct, discipline, and students' emotional support are heard and, as much as possible, addressed in concrete terms. For every teacher, these issues are antecedents to success, and sweeping them aside in the name of accepting responsibility does not appear to work. (Recall that at Stoddard School, teachers continued to be jammed up on these issues, even two full years into state intervention, and nearly every teacher complained about the state and district "just not getting it.")

Another important aspect of this stage is that it appears not to be navigable through argument or imploration. That is, the data about student performance, taken alone, are simply not a compelling reason for most teachers to reflect deeply and then to agree to sacrifice much of their autonomy and commit to coherent, schoolwide changes in teaching practice. As much as they feel they can, teachers do take their test scores seriously; they just don't all agree that improvements can be made through collegiality and mutual obligations to their peers. Moreover, gentleness, leavened with action at the school level, may be the surest way through this tempestuous developmental stage.

STAGE TWO: ADMINISTRATIVE RESPONSES TO THE CRISIS

Researchers have described a pattern in the responses of many low-performing schools as reaching for the low-hanging fruit. That is, many schools react to accountability by doubling down on what they already do, by increasing their attention to students' test-taking skills, and by providing students additional opportunities to practice the test. The administrative reaction, however, represents dysfunction—a relatively low-level response to a challenge that requires deep innovation.

Keeping in mind, though, that any low-performing school can spend years in turmoil in the wake of being labeled as underperforming, these responses may actually serve to more efficiently resolve the tough dilemmas faced by their leaders. In fact, administrative responses, which may be coupled with any number of school-level actions, represent a second, incrementally more proactive stage in the development of a low-performing school. Certainly, a school's response cannot be only administrative, but administrative actions can be as much about culture building for teachers as they are about skill building for students. The actions can help set the cultural stage: to move teachers to accept not only their role as primary agents in students' learning, but also a vision of collegiality and mutual professional obligation. This is about playing the long game, about going for short-term gains in student learning while looking for every possible advantage in the long-term development of the school.

In this stage, then, one should include a range of activities, most of which are often introduced by the school administrator: data analysis, the creation of new remedial or intensive programs, efforts to teach test-taking skills, Saturday camps, new professional development and training, the creation of pacing guides and standards-based units, and even the introduction of new programs in English or math. According to the Center on Education Policy, which conducted a survey of several hundred districts with underperforming schools, these are the most common strategies pursued by schools, anyway.[1]

As suggested by the three schools in this book, these strategies are far less frequently undertaken as a matter of deliberate developmental strategy. None of these improvement activities is new to the world of education, and none is guaranteed to produce the type of coherent, classroom-by-classroom change that sustained improvement requires. Teachers can be present for any of these activities, as nominal members of the staff, and then can just opt out. Intervention or not, administrative responses to crises in schools is the status quo in American education. Accountability and intervention, however, exacerbate, with very mixed outcomes, the tension between the leaders' needs for deep participation in, and enactment of, improvement strategies by teachers and the teachers' ability to opt out. The conflict arises partly from contractual protections, but it is far more a matter of politics: principals feel alone in their schools, teachers draw on a long history of independence in their classrooms, and any effort to affect the teaching in every classroom is considered patently political. Teachers can passively withdraw their support of an initiative or a principal. At Connington, they just chose to rebel.

So, the earliest intervention work in schools isn't about just going for the low-hanging fruit, even if schools' responses can be characterized in this stage as superficial. These early months and years are vital to a low-performing school's chances. Either school leaders will find a balanced way to resolve the fundamental dilemma between classroom improvement and stability—commiserating with the hurt feelings while engaging staff members in a conversation about, say, the quality of an after-school program—or they won't. And either they will find their own particular route through the acrimony, doubt, and deflection, with more or less efficiency, or they won't. Because this stage is deeply cultural and necessarily involves protecting teachers' professional identities with an eye for the work that will depend on their professionalism, there appears to be no shortcut through this work. The real difference is the degree to which school leaders and the people who support them understand their work as a matter of developmental strategy. If, in their view, these improvement activities are the endpoint, then one need look no further as to why intervention produces so little. If, on the other hand, school leaders view these activities as a way station to more challenging and promising work and balance the competing interests of their chief dilemmas, then schools stand to increase the chances and efficiency of their progress.

STAGE THREE: VOLUNTARISM

With the emotional reactions and administrative responses either launching or in full motion, a third stage in the improvement trajectory appears to center on the voluntarism of increasing numbers of teachers. At this stage, some teachers—the school's teacher-leaders and a handful of others—are more apt to become involved in projects that might have an impact on the *instructional core* of the school, that is, the curriculum, instruction, and assessment at the heart of teachers' ability to increase student learning. All the confusion about, and distaste for, the school's accountability status, if it has been handled well, has become less pressing, and more and more teachers see the personal advantages of their involvement in such activities as professional development, coaching, collaborative work like lesson planning and writing units, and discussions with administrators about their teaching.

In this stage, a new level of trust takes hold among most teachers, and pockets of more proficient instruction begin to take hold. In researcher Anthony Bryk's view, this trust is perhaps the single most important asset for an improving school and one that must be tended with all due care.[2] Unfortunately, intervention can destroy trust inside a school—or can induce principals to side almost dysfunctionally with their teachers, jeopardizing the productive impulse that intervention can provide. School leaders and support providers should more deliberately shepherd this currently uncontrolled outcome of intervention as part of their developmental strategy.

In a sense, this voluntarism precedes the establishment of a baseline for instructional practice in the school. A *baseline* is the point at which all the faculty can talk uniformly about the minimum expectations of the instruction they wish to deliver. There is still nothing like a set of universal expectations for teachers' practice at this stage in a school's development, but the components of a baseline can be seen in many classrooms in the school. Meetings, especially when they bring together groups of teachers with varying levels of commitment to the school's improvement activities, can be contentious, as they were at Stoddard, or just quiet, like meetings at Connington.

This stage in a school's development can be precarious: teachers who champion the efforts of reform are easily viewed as something like enemy collaborators, and others, who may be hanging back for any number of reasons, are easily regarded as resistors. These dynamics, if left unattended, can produce very damaging fissures within the faculty and represent a powerful dilemma with which school leaders will continually wrestle. Here, as in many other stages, some infusion of expertise appears critical—and is most often absent. For Stoddard, Tanner, and Connington Schools, there was no consistent assistance with governance meetings or site professional development. They were literally left on their own to develop insights about their work and to develop the content of their training. The result was the evolution of two groups with the school—the followers and the resistors—and the introduction of a troubling new dynamic within their ranks. There may be no easy way through this development, but the trouble cannot remain unnamed and the outcome of this predictable cultural development cannot be left to chance. Again, it's little wonder that intervention truly succeeds in so few cases.

Still, no school can succeed only on the strength of its volunteers. Volunteerism without a common baseline can leave students with variable learning experiences from year to year and doesn't do enough to ensure that entire cohorts of students are well taught. A baseline of instruction is necessary to establish minimum expectations. Schools set such a baseline and then enact this common commitment each day. In this way, some baseline—any baseline—is itself a milestone for schools in need of improvement. To move along new stages of development, schools should view this baseline as a constantly elevating floor.

STAGE FOUR: UNIVERSALISM AND SCHOOL IDENTITY

Despite having been labeled as an underperforming school for five years, Stoddard School never achieved a coherent approach to its work; it never managed to get all its teachers on board. Worse, it never established a baseline for what it expected of teachers in the classroom. Most intervention schools haven't yet reached this cohesiveness of their mission. The challenge of full implementation—of fidelity to a way of teaching, really—is the one thing that most schools and districts have been after, but have trouble achieving.

To judge from the experiences of the three schools in this book, there appears to be some stage between the voluntarism we saw at Stoddard, where small groups of teachers showed a heightened commitment to the school's reform agenda, and the internal accountability so critical to sustained improvement. At Connington, expectations were held universally, and broad implementation of, and fidelity to, the school's instructional programs were no longer issues. Teachers identified with their school, and everyone in the building was able to express in considerable detail the "Connington way" of going about their work. These qualities of universality and school identity are the hallmarks of a school with a strong sense of "identity practices," an indicator that some have described as critical to the development of improving schools.[3] Connington was a coherent school, with a strong mission, a high level of agreement about teaching, and common commitment to student learning. In all these respects, it was distinct from the other schools in this book.

But as the Connington case shows, even this stage, in which teachers operate with a baseline of expectations and do so uniformly, isn't the end of the road. At Connington, teachers did adhere to the same set of expectations for teaching: they followed pacing guides that they had created; administered formative assessments from the district; benefited from regular opportunities to be coached; spent time in meetings listening to the principal review these results; operated a schoolwide, flexible intervention program in mathematics and reading; and enjoyed a uniform, high level of commitment to improving the school. But still, over seven years of intervention, Connington had never satisfied the state's requirements for English language arts, and in the year of this study, it failed to meet this mark in math, too. Even with a universal approach to instruction, the school was sliding backward. In the view of its teachers, this stage of uniformity was achieved through serendipity, and it wasn't at all clear where the next promising idea would come from. Professional learning had stalled, and the school had no additional resources available to push it through these doldrums.

So, it's not enough that a school has a sense of its identity—even its instructional identity. Even though this is a massive accomplishment and one that rarely happens in American public schools, this still isn't enough. It's the difference between getting a crew to board a ship and getting them to perform all the complicated, varied tasks associated with sailing it. To make steady progress, the low-performing school needs to convert all its existing systems. It needs to move from blaming someone or something else to accepting responsibility for the outcomes it produces. It must move from very weak control of instruction to strong control that is, maybe paradoxically, distributed among all its teachers. The school must expand its attention from initiatives outside its classrooms to ones within them. And it must overcome the powerful incentives of the compliance-oriented response in favor of the far more challenging development of professional learning.

All of this is asking for something like self-actualization on an organizational level. Imagine the school in which all teachers perform every day at roughly the same level, within the boundaries of a joint definition of good instruction—*and then expand this mutual practice in response to information about the results of this work.* This is nothing easy. This is asking every school to be exceptional. And so far, we've been asking schools to do this without any attention at all to how this could be done.

STAGE FIVE: INTERNAL ACCOUNTABILITY AND SUSTAINED GROWTH

The end game for schools, low-performing or otherwise, is this: that all teachers agree to and frequently enact a common understanding of powerful teaching practice and learn together so that this understanding is adaptive, conscious, and expanding. None of the schools in this book succeeded in attaining this last stage. They failed to develop mutual expectations or to push ahead in any coherent way on the basis of what they were learning about their struggling students. No school could thoughtfully incorporate new ideas into a solid base of practice. Connington got the closest, to be sure, but ahead of it lay the formidable task of repairing the damage done to the trust between the principal and his staff. Joint learning was still a long way off.

Setting the school improvement compass toward internal accountability represents a significant departure from intervention as we've seen it so far. In particular, the idea that teachers will help reinforce expectations for professional practice—rather than being subject to this reinforcement by some external authority—is the greatest distance left to travel. For this kind of mutuality to occur, there's got to be trust between everyone on the team: between teachers and their colleagues, between staff members and their principal, between schools and their districts. Everyone needs to have faith in teachers' ability to discern good and bad teaching and to modify their practices in response to the outcomes they produce. Well beyond just knowing that a teacher won't be punished by a principal for not getting on board, this kind of trust means a faith in teachers' professional discretion—the type of discretion a competent professional might exercise within a well-defined framework of what usually works for students. For most of the teachers in this book, this kind of trust hadn't yet become part of what they understood as possible. In these schools, as in most low-performing school, discretion was something one was either allowed by a principal or not. It was an absolute, an either-or proposition. No one at Stoddard, Tanner, or Connington believed that a teacher could choose how to teach, using a limited set of higher-power strategies. And of course, none of the principals in this book had reason to be entirely confident that their teachers' unbridled discretion was warranted. The instructional baseline was just too low.

But if Connington School got farthest along the path to internal accountability, what was it still missing? Buy-in was no longer the problem at this school; neither was an unacceptably high variation in the quality of the teaching. But still, the school was stuck. To better understand what internal accountability looks like, let's look at what could have jolted Connington out of its rut and moved it forward again.

First, Connington hadn't yet developed a meaningful mechanism for asking and answering a more refined set of questions about teaching and learning. Teachers in this school understood that they weren't being as effective as they wanted, even with fairly high fidelity to the reforms they had adopted. But they had no idea what to do next and no reasonable way to locate their next steps. They appeared unable to pose an actionable question about what problem they needed to solve, and then they had no resources—either in the form of a person or team with both time and expertise—to go out beyond the school's walls to look for an answer. Jesse Martinez, the principal who brought an instructional identity to the school mostly by force, was now banking on the creativity of his tremulous staff as the source of the next breakthrough. The teachers hoped their weekend reading might suffice. This wasn't exactly the system for joint professional learning and problem solving that the school needed, and it illustrates perfectly the challenges of moving toward internal accountability.

To move into this last, most promising developmental stage, Connington School needed all its gears to touch and move. It needed a district apparatus in tune with its particular needs, with people whose skills suited the school's challenges. The school essentially needed someone to design and lead research—someone who could pose a question about the patterns in student learning produced by their school and then identify the training, idea, or program with the best chance of improving this pattern. Clearly, this was outside the job description of a classroom teacher or a principal. The task was so far beyond what Connington could be expected to do by itself that the school just might not ever get any further.

Second, Connington had no way to fine-tune its meetings to match the learning needs of all its teachers. Like so many urban schools, this was an amalgam staff, with a mix of veteran and novice teachers, each with a wide array of skills. And now firmly settled into a 25 percent turnover rate each year, Connington needed an efficient induction mechanism, a way of helping its young teachers master the basics of classroom management and the advances its other teachers had made over the last seven years. At the same time, the school also needed a way to support its more knowledgeable staff members, those who had come to Connington because they were as ambitious and skilled as Martinez, but who had now played all their cards. In common educational terms, there was no differentiation at Connington, and the lack of year-by-year attention to the capacities of the staff—as individuals and as a group—contributed to everyone's sense that they were stuck.

If Connington tried to make the next steps toward improvement—one step further toward internal accountability and progressively greater gains in student learning—the school's isolation would clearly hurt the cause. This work cannot be done without substantial support, especially for an average low-performing school, with its predictable tableau of ongoing student crises, staff turnover, hardball politics, and impenetrable bureaucracy. In fact, no strategy discussed so far would be likely to move such schools to this most advanced developmental stage. Without major additional support for these schools, the changes of success would be slim.

In summary, building the features of internal accountability for any school isn't at all easy—especially considering the difficult path from low-performing to high-performing schools. But the real challenge isn't so much in describing what a few outlier schools are doing or in mapping backward from these descriptions. It's how real schools, with real teachers—all the thousands of them across the country—begin to navigate the tricky course in this direction, one tough dilemma at a time. This work always runs counter to most school culture, but not so much that everything falls apart. In contrast to what current intervention has been delivering, this requires an awareness of school development, an explicit strategy based on this awareness, and ongoing, developmental guidance about how to resolve difficult problems with the long game in mind.

Thoughtful teacher-leaders, principals, superintendents, and policy makers need to ask how we all can kick the habit of pretending that this work is easier than it really is. What systems should we build, now that we have state testing systems and accountability labels? If the goal is to create quality public education in places where it hasn't existed—and not just undermine public confidence to the point that the whole system is destroyed, as it sometimes feels—then what are the implications of all the information this chapter? How do we take what we know about the stages of development in low-performing schools and build a system for its use?

To envision a developmental approach to school intervention, we must wrestle with the features of these schools and of the larger organizations in which they exist. To really make use of these ideas, widening the scope to include school, district, and state is essential. The profound isolation of these schools lies at the heart of the inefficiencies, and this isolation is only worsened if we talk exclusively about what low-performing schools need to do. Making room for thoughtfulness and discernment requires a broader view than this.

In the last chapter of this book, we turn our attention from how to understand the needs of a particular low-performing school to how to best match these needs with meaningful support. This work, both conceptual and practical, necessarily involves looking at the common structures and practices that leave so many schools without the help they need. The next generation of intervention in low-performing schools consequently must rise from more solid ground. When low-performing schools have policy that is grounded in their own reality, everyone involved in the turnaround enterprise dramatically increases the odds of success in this vitally important work.

6

Twelve Steps Toward Supporting Struggling Schools

I n discussing what appeared to be going wrong in the three under-performing schools, the book has so far necessarily focused on the cultural, political, and organizational hurdles these schools face. None of the schools exhibited any awareness of its larger developmental trajectory or had anything like a developmental strategy as it faced down its daily dilemmas. Every underperforming school will possess, in its details, similar school-level challenges. If a developmental strategy was missing, and this absence led to missed opportunities, cyclical efforts, and eventually something like quicksand, it begs the question of what can be done. What are the levers? On what set of enriched principles should a new system of support be predicated? How do we improve the odds that low-performing schools resolve their core dilemmas so that they travel toward sustained academic growth more efficiently?

To answer these questions means looking inside the schools themselves—it means knowing these schools better, accounting for the foundational facts of their existence, and doing a better job of matching needs to resources. None of these things are features of current intervention systems. Answering these questions also means looking at the institutions and structures that surround and prop up—and often constrain—the low-performing schools that are the targets of state accountability. These institutions often have as little strategy about, and awareness of, the development of low-performing schools as the schools do themselves. Problem solving and collaborative learning are not the values that carry the day.

In chapter 5, which discusses the putting together of a developmental profile for low-performing schools, we considered the question of just what we should know about low-performing schools—developmental information that goes well beyond a single-number aggregation of testing data and a straight count of the number of years the school has missed its performance targets. We saw that knowing something about the school's orientation toward a few key, predictable dilemmas can matter a great deal, especially when low-performing schools, in their great isolation, somehow manage these dilemmas with so much inefficiency. There is presently enough knowledge about the stages of school development to locate schools somewhere on the path to internal accountability. If not an exact science, the knowledge is more than enough to improve on the one-size-fits-all approach that we've so far used, with insufficient effect, on this population of schools.

The overarching need for a developmental strategy in low-performing schools, however, is that the requirements and support of intervention, as they are delivered over a period of years, should match the evolving developmental needs of the school.

The rest of this chapter outlines what developmental support could have been offered to the three schools or to any underperforming school. Twelve suggestions are offered, with specific ways to implement them.

1. Stage Implementation

As a counterpoint for how intervention is currently viewed, interventions might better be conceived of as staged implementations, where relatively low-level problems like the formation of remedial programs are tackled as a matter of strategy and, critically, as a means for building the capacity needed for focusing on problems of classroom practice. As the school's profile develops and as it increasingly resolves its dilemmas in ways that focus more on classroom instruction while maintaining stability, the stages of implementation should become more refined, more focused on developing teachers' skills and common high-level expectations. With a far higher probability, schools with meaningful developmental support will resolve their dilemmas in ways that move them incrementally closer to a fully realized form of internal accountability. In fact, intervention policy should assume that these schools' profiles will change over time, while at the same time acknowledging that the level of support they require will not diminish. The experience of Connington and Stoddard, however, suggested the opposite: because the problems only became harder over time, the sophistication of the support needed to correspond to these complications. These schools' experiences are consistent with the research findings that low-performing schools are often capable of their hardest and most promising work only after struggling through an initial period of marginal improvements.

Clearly missing in the experiences of these schools was any effort to help school leaders think developmentally about their schools, with some set of long-term goals about how to organize the school, what teachers should do, and which of these goals should generally come first. No one in any of these schools had thought about a long-range plan. District leaders, principals, and teachers received no support for this kind of learning, and in the absence of even a theory of how each school might improve over time, each year's decision making was little more than simple reaction.

Obviously, there is no prescription or formula for a developmental approach to intervention. In fact, this book argues that we've so far relied to heavily on prescriptions—and with very meager results. With the wisdom we can gain from thoughtful reflection, however, there are some signposts. Better than insisting on the same initial steps for every school, for example, intervention should start by putting together a developmental profile based on what is known about the trajectory of schools that have walked this path. Better than decentralizing responsibility while constraining choice, effective intervention would organize for joint learning. Better than isolation is collaboration. We may not have a road map, but we're beginning to understand the contours.

The concept of staged intervention supposes that certain improvement activities make more sense than others—and that a school's executive team, with information, can make decisions that are more strategic than those made by a lockstep set of mandates. Schools need to track multiple measures: the gains that they hope will come from short-term fix-ups like after-school programs; the level of collegiality among staff; the extent to which teachers trust administration; the school's tolerance for some instability; or the effects of individual decisions on the prospects for achieving something like internal accountability. Though the list of possible improvement activities is long, most schools, like the three in this book, try to do them all—and then get very few of them right. A staged intervention values strategy, quality, and cumulative professional growth.

2. Get Serious About Collaboration and Problem Solving

Taking a developmental approach to intervening in low-performing schools will require that everyone involved in the enterprise, from schools to district offices to state departments of education, gets serious about collaborative learning and problem solving—mainly because it looks as though this is the *only* way forward for these schools. This isn't a matter of philosophy; it's a matter of necessity. The dilemmas described in chapter 5, when resolved by principals and teachers in isolation and only in the context of their own schools, too often will lead schools back into the quicksand. The tug toward stability is so powerful, and the rules in American schools are so stacked against classroom-by-classroom improvements in teaching practices, that any informed observer should assume that stability is the course most schools will pursue—even in the face of seemingly compelling sanctions.

To counter this, support providers must get themselves organized to know their target schools more deeply. Intervention must infuse schools with more expert and explicit knowledge about how organizations like theirs develop, and target schools need ongoing, matched guidance so that the predictable dilemmas that are exacerbated by intervention are resolved in ways that move schools along as efficient a path as possible. Breaking the norm is no easy task, and no norm or group should escape scrutiny for how it supports or impedes these necessary counteractions.

Though straightforward enough as concepts, neither staged implementation nor joint professional learning occupies any place in the current conception of how to help low-performing schools get better. And more important, only when these ideas are turned into practicable systems will they have any power to break the long, inefficient cycles such as those at Stoddard, Tanner, and Connington. Staged implementation and joint professional development can break schools' isolation with consistent, well-matched infusions of expertise about organizational development and increasingly sophisticated pedagogy. The point is to break the very common, random execution of improvement activities by developing a developmental strategy for each school, one that will guide all the educators who labor toward the betterment of the school. Finally, the next generation of school intervention demonstrates that incentives and sanctions alone can never adequately address a problem that is fundamentally about professional learning. At its core, school intervention must enrich schools' capacity to think strategically about their development and to view each of their improvement endeavors—whether they relate to using data, selecting professional development, or creating test-preparation programs—as a means of developing their organizations.

The following sections draw from research and the three cases presented in this book to describe serious staged implementation and collaborative problem-solving at the district and state levels, all in support of a developmental form of intervention. In the main, the list comprises long-standing institutional practices that take more than they give and to which this new set of principles should be applied. To create and follow a developmental strategy, schools and districts—especially districts—must get serious about solving the organizational, administrative, and communication problems that cripple so many low-performing schools. As schools begin to pass through the initial stages of their development, creating after-school programs or test-preparation classes, for example, support providers must anticipate that their role will only become more complex, more knowledge intensive, and more necessary. This is the direct opposite tack of what's most commonly done. Rather than assume that support can be lessened after some relatively brief period of setting new requirements for low-performing schools, support providers must rethink the catalog of intervention activities and their timeline. The activities must match the developmental strategy for each school and should be continually revised in an ongoing dialogue between schools and their support providers, as each institution makes progress on a range of indicators.

3. Ensure a Solid Instructional Foundation

Too often in low-performing schools, professional development has little chance of taking hold, because there's been no substantial work to build the foundation for instructional improvement. This was the case at Stoddard and Tanner Schools, where the district had never established any common pacing guides, assessments, or essential standards, and it's doubtless the case in other low-performing schools all over the country. At Stoddard and Tanner, teachers and principals spent their time in constant, low-level conversation about what to teach and when—about what story from the literature anthology should come next or about coordinating the start of the sixth chapter from the algebra text. Rather than carefully reflecting about teaching and learning, these schools used up their valuable time on nearly meaningless topics. In a game that's all about professional learning, these schools couldn't even field a team.

In essence, the district offices for Stoddard and Tanner blew a critical piece of their job. By opting not to create a foundation for good teaching, they missed one way to support schools in the development of more meaningful conversations about instruction. For schools still positioned far from internal accountability, like Stoddard and Tanner, it could be years before teachers find the time, the skill, and the inclination to create these resources. In fact, some schools go years—the entire length of a program adoption—without ever working from basic agreements about what is taught, when it's taught, and how it's assessed. All of this only ensures that schools remain stuck.

Instructional foundation is the relatively simple resources that form the necessary base for any type of professional, on-site learning: the pacing guides that serve as markers for the tempo of instruction; the common, regular, and standards-based assessments that ground teachers at frequent intervals in the results of their work; the key essential standards that show up most often on state tests. If these resources seem basic, it's because they truly are; on their own, they won't lead to high-quality practice in every room in a school. But they're too often missing from low-performing schools, and they are just time-intensive enough that most schools cannot create them on their own. And schools shouldn't have to.

In some districts, the instructional foundation also includes the centralized development and distribution of lesson plans—collaboratively developed descriptions of how to use a particular program to greatest effect. This is itself a form of professional development for the groups of teachers involved; writing lessons with colleagues—lesson study—is arguably an essential part of every teacher's experience at work. All this foundation, however, is about supporting—and jump-starting—the organized improvement of instruction in schools with no history of this work. As a starting point, high-quality lesson plans can also be an important part of this foundation.

Another district-level effort with the promise of benefiting schools far from internal accountability is the joint creation of classroom learning objectives. This is different from posting standards on the blackboard, a practice required of teachers in many low-performing schools and one that stands as the most potent emblem of just how autocratic—and stupid—accountability has become. Good learning objectives, when made explicit and actually used during a lesson, can make students' learning more concrete. The objectives help teachers to make the content of their lesson align with the standards for student learning and to create at least one *assessment moment* in every lesson—one instant in which they can really see what students have learned as a result of their teaching. This kind of regular assessment, and then taking action to address students' real needs, is one hallmark of expert practice, and districts can have an important role in girding this work.

One irony in the current formulation of state intervention is that low-performing schools are often required to change out the materials they've been using, substituting one state-approved textbook for another. In the process, though, a lot of this foundation—the pacing guides, the regular assessments, and so forth—isn't refreshed. As a result, low-performing schools, if they had these resources at their command in the first place, might actually take steps backward; they might fall deeper into disorganization. For this reason, the traditional sequence of steps for adopting materials—which usually takes the form of adoption committees, large orders in the spring, and summer deliveries to schools—is only a small part of the work that districts must perform. Maintaining an adequate base for professional growth also requires that districts be equally deliberate about the simultaneous refreshing of the instructional foundation.

4. Reduce the Effects of Central Office Silos

In most school districts in this country, the raft of categorical funding sources that make up a good measure of local education funds has also given rise to highly differentiated administrative offices. Each of these offices is responsible for designing, implementing, and monitoring programs that relate generally to particular groups of children—English language learners (ELLs), special education students, or intervention kids, to name a few examples—or subject areas, like English or math. The design allows for easy reporting and does support the development of some expertise about the issues affecting each of these areas. In schools, however, and in low-performing schools in particular, the distribution of responsibilities into such silos can often create additional complexity. Principals and teachers, who invariably work with groups of students with wide ranges of abilities and who are rightly asked to be concerned with high-quality *first* instruction for all students, face the challenge of integrating many district initiatives during the same class, the same lesson, and the same hour of teaching. Because the quality of first instruction (i.e., the first time that students experience new content) really counts, this is where districts and support provider should focus their attention. For the educators in classrooms, the work centers on the class, and the challenge—the way forward—is largely about how effectively they differentiate a single lesson for a wide range of learners. The work of synthesizing a district's many initiatives into a single high-quality lesson (or high-quality day or high-quality year) falls to the classroom teacher, even if it's rarely discussed. For most of the teachers in this book, the work was immensely complicated, involving many nuanced decisions about their professional practice. And remarkably, this work went entirely unexamined.

In some respects, the existence of central office silos has resulted in a problem of different languages: teachers speak in terms of classes, lessons, and units, while central office staff talk about programs and subgroups. As authors like Jennifer O'Day explain, it's a disconnect between using schools as the unit of accountability and teachers' obligations to individual students.[1] It's certainly not that one group isn't concerned about the responsibilities of the other. But the responsibilities are different, and in a situation in which low-performing schools need desperately to bend their historical isolation toward collaboration, this language problem lends little to the effort. For this reason, teachers at the Stoddard, Tanner, and Connington schools all felt, with equal uniformity, that their central office colleagues were woefully out of touch with their needs. The common refrain among them is that their districts "just don't get it."

To combat this disconnect, districts must sufficiently deconstruct their categorical silos so that responsibilities are more defined in terms of schools, and not only programs. If principals are expected to manage their multiple-site programs—math, English, ELL, special education students, after-school intervention classes—with enough acumen to lead teachers toward accomplished practice, at least some other members of the larger organization ought to share this expertise. This begs for some form of reorganization, from the school up, so that districts are able to field school-specific executive teams composed of teacher-leaders, the principal, district staff, and any other support providers. The priorities of these executive teams should be defined in terms of knowing individual schools, creating a developmental strategy, and then providing ongoing, well-matched coaching, feedback, and expertise to school leaders. Clearly, if responsibility in the accountability system is defined in terms of the individual school, then responsibility should, at least in part, also be defined in these terms for district personnel.

5. Integrate All Instructional Initiatives into One Model of Powerful Teaching

One irony of the silo structure of so many big central offices is that for many low-performing schools, the central offices has no way to operationalize the attention given to student subgroups. That is, the central office structure does not allow for practically supporting so many different groups of students into an hour of teaching. As much as a district director for special education may work for the betterment of these students alone, a teacher must work with this specific group in the context of a diverse classroom. As much as an ELL department is required to serve its clientele—in compliance with federal and state laws and often within the strictures of a local lawsuit—a teacher must work these teaching strategies into Monday's math lesson. For the average well-meaning, time-starved classroom teacher, attention is given on the basis of need, not on skin color or language group or family income. The development of all these mechanisms for preventing historical abuse wasn't unnecessary, or isn't unnecessary now. But the mechanisms make less sense on the ground level, when the attention finally shifts to high-quality lessons in every room, on every day of the week.

Teachers might point out that performance isn't correlated with demographics in the simple way that most central office organization charts suggest—at least not when most of the class is struggling during a math lesson. If teachers must conquer the intellectual challenge of creating a meaningful synthesis of many promising district initiatives so that they all take shape during a lesson, say, during math on Monday, why is this challenge left to teachers to perform on their own? Districts have a powerful role to play in defining what good lessons can and should look like, but this power only arises when district staff can see from one silo to another in order to synchronize a single, powerful instructional vision.

Low-performing schools need fewer initiatives and less cross-talk from the central office, however well intentioned it all is. For a good teacher, instructional improvement efforts in the areas of special education, ELL, or low-income students (to name a few) have far more in common than not. Even across programs—from sheltered to special education to GATE (gifted and talented education)—the approaches for supporting these different student groups rely on many of the same techniques and draw from much of the same research. Good lessons in one program share a huge amount with good lessons in the next. The emphasis is on high-quality content, with high-quality delivery and support, gauged regularly by high-quality assessment. The work of instructional improvement is mostly the same for every student, despite central offices' longtime organization to the contrary.

Given that the long-term goal for low-performing schools is a good teacher in every classroom, it makes sense to pull together the best of each of these many instructional models. What's more, every support provider needs to start to talk about all this work in the language of the classroom: in terms of the beginning, middle, and end of effective lessons; in uniform definitions of a well-crafted unit; in terms of revealing formative assessments. Though this approach works for all schools, it is especially important for schools in long-standing distress. Schools in trouble need everyone on the same page, and we now know more than enough about effective classroom teaching—for all students—to settle for anything less than this.

6. Create Reciprocal Improvement Planning

At Stoddard and Connington Schools, improvement planning was one of three key elements in the state's efforts to produce a turnaround. The beefed-up plans mainly reflected the requirements for describing the schools' test data and acted as an indicator for central office and state monitors that the schools had selected a new set of improvement activities. At ground level, however, the plans were widely regarded as artifacts of a new emphasis on compliance; they were symbols of reduced autonomy and trust. And most certainly, they were not viewed as written reflections of a dialogue between the school and its monitors. The plans were written by the principal or a small group; they largely reflected what the schools already did or the unimproved knowledge base of the people who wrote them. As with most improvement plans, which are nothing new to American education, the obligations encoded in these plans mostly flowed from the school to the district.[2] In effect, these plans reduced the visibility of any differences between low-performing schools in the same district and correspondingly reduced the chance that the district would be aware of the dilemmas and challenges these schools were trying to solve on their own.

Clearly, neither Stoddard nor Connington gained much by participating in the improvement planning ritual. The process garnered little attention in the schools, because most teachers already knew the deal: the plans weren't for real. They had never been for real, and intervention didn't change this situation. In the years prior to the state's efforts to intervene in low-performing schools, improvement planning was a decidedly low-impact event.[2] In the throes of intervention, however, the year's plan remained at the farthest margins of most teachers' attention.

None of this means that improvement planning is unimportant, of course. But some adaptations are necessary, ones that will support a new set of principles about intervention. Improvement planning needs to reduce isolation, not reinforce this state; it needs to support a developmental knowledge of individual schools, not assuming that every low-performing school is the same. In addition to creating a developmental profile for each school, which should form the basis of a jointly constructed executive strategy, planning must become a reciprocal activity. That is, improvement planning should provide a school district with the information it needs to define its own priorities—essentially, the process should provide enough data to district staff so that their services to schools can be differentiated by need. Rather than rely exclusively on the top-down planning so typical in most school districts—the board sets the goals, the districts relay them to schools, and the schools mechanically write them into their plans—school-level planning should provide the occasion in which information can move "up" the system.

This is a decidedly "classroom-like" way to organize the work of struggling schools. In fact, it directly parallels what good teachers do: they plan for instruction according to what they consider the strengths and weaknesses of the students in their class. They group students in flexible and strategic ways. They rely heavily on data to make adjustments to their plans, but it's mostly data about what students have learned in response to a lesson or a unit. Yearly data, measuring a circumscribed set of skills, is necessary, but alone it's just not sufficient support for accomplished practice. There is high degree of reciprocity in this model: good teachers respond just as much as their students do. The same should be true of effective school districts, and as far off as we are right now from anything like this, school planning should be the cornerstone of this kind of reciprocity. Remember, isolation and inattention to the variations in low-performing schools are the broken cogs in intervention today. School improvement planning should serve as a tool in the repair kit.

7. Bust Up the Principalship

One need only read the cases in this book to see how central principals are to the success of their schools. They are the lynchpins, and for better or worse, no other individual has as much impact on any effort at intervention. There's no way to make school turnaround a principal-proof project. Why, then, has so important a task as intervention—one in which the educational outcomes of many thousands of children lie in the balance—brought so little change to the fundamental, very well documented isolation and overload of the position of principal? Why has the principalship, the critical component in the intervention formula, merited no substantial rethinking so far?

The experiences at the Stoddard, Tanner, and Connington schools make as clear as the literature does just how important principals are. Principals can accelerate the pace of change or bring it to a halt. They can enhance the substance of the state's purposes or chase an entire staff out of the school. They can resist change and maybe keep themselves well allied with their faculty, or they can lead a charge toward enriched professional learning. In just the three schools we've seen, principals have done all these things. And they probably could have taken any of these paths, because nobody was really paying attention—either to their professional isolation or to how intervention had only exacerbated the dilemmas at their particular schools. This leaves the principals' personal style, personal philosophy, and personal courage—none of which can be quantified or systematized—as massive determinants in the success of each intervention effort.

In the end, of course, there is no such thing as people-proof reform in schools. Whatever intervention you introduce to a school, you're almost always talking about the same group of teachers serving the same group of children, in the same number of hours, in the same building, with the same basic working conditions. At the very least, the principals at Stoddard, Tanner, and Connington first needed some acknowledgement that the work really would test their discernment, their judgment, and their ability to persuade. They needed support for this part of their work, and not just exhortation. More practically, they also needed some reduction in the crush of daily responsibilities that allowed them—or forced them—to rank instructional leadership as less important than operational needs. Given the needs and the urgency of the school's crisis, it just didn't make sense that the Stoddard's principal had to deliver his school's mail by 3:30 every afternoon. This single, absurd requirement at the Stoddard could easily symbolize what was wrong with nearly everyone's view of the principal's job. None of the three schools had done any policy-level thinking about the effect of all the operational tasks—so many of which amount to delivering the school's mail by hand—that had so effectively and for so long competed for principals' time.

If a new generation of intervention must start by fixing the problems of isolation and the widespread inattention to the problem-solving skills required of target schools, it follows that principals must be substantially unfettered. The principalship should be broken up. Into one group of responsibilities should go mission-critical tasks like daily school walk-throughs; regular feedback for teachers; evaluation; mentoring new teachers; the organization of and dogged follow-up on professional development; quality assurance of faculty, department, or grade-level meetings; understanding and acting on assessment data; and meeting with school support providers. Into the other bailiwick go the tasks related to almost everything else: budgets, requisitions, campus upkeep, attendance, transportation, report writing, and any other symbolic equivalent of delivering the mail. In most schools—even intervention schools in which significant sanctions have been brought to bear—the two groups of responsibilities are assigned with equal weight only to principals, and the results so far are just what you'd expect. Future intervention can thus either continue to bank on the magnanimity and skill of superhero principals or do something to fix this problem; it can move away from a twentieth-century construction of a position that looks utterly unsuitable for twenty-first-century education.

Maddeningly, the solution is mostly a function of just creating a new position to handle all the scut work, something like an empowered administrative assistant—probably at only a third the cost of a principal's salary. It might be the most important way to fix the dysfunction near the heart of so many low-performing schools. In the other, potentially more promising solution, the school hands over the list of instructional improvement activities to someone who knows even more about them than the average principal. This director of instruction has the know-how, the authority (in the form of an administrator's title), and the *time* to get the work done.

After a century or so of the same organizational structure in public schools, we know that the clay has pretty well hardened on the principal's role. Parents, teachers, students, and central office workers all have very fixed interpretations of what a principal should do, and all continue to make the same demands on the people in these positions. Under these old, entrenched attitudes, parent meetings, e-mails from the food service department about kids who didn't eat, requests for information from the superintendent's office, parking problems, student fights, and parent complaints—all coming at the average principal with great consistency, each one legitimately representing someone else's emergency—come to outweigh the daily task of improving teaching. In fact, this is just obvious; the principalship in most low-performing schools is a staffing issue. And whatever the solution, the goal is to substantially separate out the many tasks related to instructional improvement from everything else. This work should be harbored from all the rogue waves and riptides that make up life in a low-performing school.

8. Organize People and Time at the Earliest Stage

At Stoddard School, performance improvement mapping (PIM) introduced in very short order a brand new way to organize the school and conduct business—even if this business was immediately compromised by staff politics and home-spun remedies. Completely in contrast, Tanner, with its monthly faculty meetings and dependence on substitute teachers to release grade-level teams, had no similarly effective way to organize people and time, and nothing on the horizon looked as though it would affect this arrangement. This important deficit in Tanner's infrastructure could limit the reach of its efforts long into the future. In light of this, Stoddard's establishment of an organized decision-making structure through PIM brought considerable value. This aspect of the intervention should probably have come far sooner for Stoddard—even in the first year of the school's status as underperforming and even if the content of its early meetings had little to do with the improvement of classroom teaching.

Along with the development of a meaningful school profile, the introduction of structures for organizing time and people appears to be essential and should be included as one of the first few steps taken by an external authority trying to help improve a low-performing school. The creation of time for meetings and trainings might be the most expensive proposition in this book, because every hour of teachers' time away from students adds cost to schools, either in the form of salary stipends or additional personnel to cover classrooms, but it's almost impossible to conceive of improvement in low-performing schools without this investment in infrastructure.

Of course, making sure that low-performing schools have the time and organizational structures to support professional learning over the long term is in itself insufficient. The teacher-leaders and principal at Connington School had frequent meetings, but were still deeply stuck; they found themselves banking on serendipity as the source of their next good idea. Intervention's emphasis on creating the time and teams upon which professional learning will eventually rest must also include central office staffers and state support providers. Responsibilities for central office staffers should adhere as much to the success of low-performing schools as they do to departments or programs. Jointly constructed executive teams for each school should know about the developmental pathways for low-performing schools and should be expected to develop expertise related to these needs, too. The formation of teams clearly isn't the key to success, but it's one important antidote to the isolation and inflexibility that confront low-performing schools.

The next generation of intervention should act far more quickly to remedy the absence of professional learning time in these schools; to do otherwise is to build a house on a foundation of sand.

9. Focus on District Inefficiencies

Curiously, the current drive toward charter schools—call it the effort to find a detour around the morass of traditional public education—pays scarce corresponding attention to the role of classified unions in supporting school performance. The current U.S. Department of Education is expressing its willingness to pull the plug on many schools, either in the form of school closures or fire-sale giveaways to charter organizations. The target in these efforts, quite clearly, is ineffective management, whether it is defined as the lack of options about moving poor teachers out, other overly restrictive contract provisions, weak principals, or chronic disorganization. Getting away from the mess in favor of nearly anything else is still a movement in the making.

This chapter is about the remaking of the relationship between low-performing schools and their supporters, including district offices. For too many low-performing schools, these relationships are truly dysfunctional, and the schools burn countless reserves trying accomplish their basic daily functions: student transportation, food services, technology, student assignment, student services, special education, and so forth. When these things, and a hundred others, aren't working well, you can forget about any consistent attention to teaching and learning. You can forget about instructional leadership. If it were a business running itself this way, with its success tied to efficiency, customer service, and the bottom line, it wouldn't last a year.

Principal Jesse Martinez of Connington School described much of this dysfunction in his reasoned analysis of his district. How can he succeed, he asked privately, if the district skims the top third of his students each year so that it can fill the advanced placement program down the street? How can he succeed when his school is the redirect location for every over-enrolled school in his zone? How will he make it work when his ELL and self-contained programs grow by one classroom per year, or when he's forced to take the involuntary transfer teacher bounced from ten schools in as many years? What about the purchase requisitions that take five phone calls apiece or a trip to the purchasing department? The routine plant maintenance that takes weeks to complete? The custodian he has to pay at time-and-a-half from his own budget every time Martinez opens his school to families on a Saturday? Martinez had his stories, and so did Trisha Waighn and Ken Schumer. For instance, Schumer's required afternoon trips to pick up his school mail on the other side of town would make you laugh if the whole thing didn't make you cry.

Of course, some of this is beyond fixing. In systems the size of most big school districts, with a century-long history of progressive labor reforms designed to prevent graft and favoritism, all the routines, both effective and dysfunctional, are very fixed. But there is work to be done, and district leaders are on the hook for beginning to think ruthlessly about locating and eliminating inefficiencies. They should start by thinking hard about the inefficiencies that come from having a weak or nonexistent instructional foundation. They should also examine the effect of all the cross-talk about teaching—all the competing initiatives coming from categorical programs that have to take seed in the same garden, anyway. These are the biggest inefficiencies faced by the three schools in this book. Because they are also common enough in most other places, they should be considered in the overall design of state intervention, as should some analysis of how principals are required to spend their time in order to accomplish the basic tasks of running their schools. If schools are to be treated developmentally and supported to grow over time, improvement can't be expected to happen without dismantling some of the offending inefficiencies.

10. Create Data About Learning—And About Practice

The schools in this book also clearly struggled to connect performance data to classroom practice. Teachers in all the schools struggled with the timeliness of the data they had, with what they saw as confusing year-to-year variations in the data, with the fact that they no longer taught the students whose results they were given, and with the disconnect between the data and the instructional programs they were required to follow. What did make a difference, at least at Connington School, was the existence of regular, organized, and valid measures of student learning that could more easily be connected to classroom practice. These formative assessment data came from the central office and the large federal reading grant the school received. In combination with the robust team structure of the school, all this additional information put Connington in the strongest position of the three schools to make rational, incremental improvements to teachers' work. In effect, the formative data were another critical feature of the school's infrastructure; even though the school wasn't out of the woods, its formative assessment system was a cornerstone in the school's ongoing efforts to get better.

Beyond just having the data, however, all three schools had problems with how they acted on their conclusions about the data. Most authors who write about using data in schools emphasize the importance of a school staff's ability to construct reasonable hypotheses about the data it collects; in fact, the quality of these hypotheses appear to be directly related to the quality of the staff's decision making in other areas.[3] A staff that tends to associate poor student performance with factors out of its control may not find in the data any compelling challenge to its current practices.

But what happens in a school where teachers are able to collect valid data, analyze these data, and bring to their analysis a set of beliefs that lead the school to focus on what it can control? How do schools select the best instructional strategies in response to the data—the practices that are most likely to succeed? One helpful clue comes from a 2001 report by Education Commission of the States. The group reports that schools must maintain and develop a "bank" of knowledge about best practices through a consistent reading of instructional research and access to professional development as part of an assessment cycle.[4] In other words, besides conducting reasonably accurate analyses of their data, schools must also have access to sufficient instructional expertise—a databank of ideas and strategies. Low-performing schools need help matching their observations about what's needed with effective strategies devised by those outside the school. Maintaining this bank of promising practices is clearly in the purview of states and districts and lies well beyond the capabilities of most low-performing schools. Getting the ideas into low-performing schools, where few people have the time to read research and where there is certainly no systematic approach to pulling in new ideas, should be a design feature of the next generation of intervention.

Information, then, has a lot to do with setting the stage for serious collaborative learning and problem solving, but not quite in the way that many people think. For schools in the earliest stages of their development—and maybe for any school that hasn't yet established a baseline of common practice for all its teachers—information about practice may have more power than information about learning. Information about practice is more useful, primarily because the challenge in these schools is implementation—coherent, classroom-by-classroom implementation. The challenge is not yet about adaptation. These schools just aren't the data-based, rational, adaptive institutions so often described in the literature. This adaptable, data-based rationality is the goal, however, and so the ground must be tilled as a part of intervention. The creation of information systems will eventually support the adjustment of instruction, and a databank of practice will enable teachers to make more informed responses to information about learning.

Finally, none of the schools had any means of collecting what might be called input data, that is, consistent, reliable information about what was going on in their classrooms. Remarkably, the Stoddard leadership team wrote its state-approved plan, with all its conjecture about the root causes of students' poor performance, without ever having visited another teacher's classroom. They could only rely on their impressions of the classes down the hall, and really, they had no idea what corrections were needed. To say that data use has value, after all, assumes the existence of a basic system, with some combination of inputs leading to some set of outcomes. In most low-performing schools, the people who make decisions have access to information only about the last half of this function, the outcome. In other words, they're able to dress up their guesses with numbers—but without reliable knowledge of either the quantity or quality of what the school actually delivers, the decisions can't be anything but guesses.

A serious approach to collaborative learning and problem solving has to address this deficit of input information as well—however countercultural the idea may be to most schools. There's just no way around the schools' need to know, even in quantitative terms, what students experience during instruction. For example, how could a low-performing school know if replacing its math program makes sense if no one knows specifically whether its key components are even in regular use? If no one bothers to ask such a basic question, and if intervention design doesn't support the collection of information that could answer it, then low-performing schools will just keep guessing.

11. Educate the Politicians

One powerful theme the three schools shared was just how susceptible they were to all the various sources of instability in their environment and how the capacity of various groups and individuals to create this instability gave rise to so much small-scale politics. Principals and teacher-leaders, the main protagonists in these political stories, made all kinds of decisions to keep the peace. In fact, there really was no "technical" side to intervention at all. The data, the planning, the monitoring— all of it—was ultimately about the politics of the school.

It's no secret that public schools in America are attached at the hip to local politics. The dynamic, enshrined in the institution of the school board, is both a strength and a weakness. The average school board, with its regular elections, is sufficiently robust to endure runs by extreme elements in a community and sensitive enough to local predilections that it can make sustained, multiyear efforts almost impossible. The Kansas school board that wrote evolution out of its curriculum reversed this decision a few years later, once a new slate of board members had been voted in.

The Boston Public Schools had a fruitful ten-year run at reform under Tom Payzant, largely because through that period, the district's school committee was appointed by Mayor Tom Menino. Boston's example, however, is more the exception than the rule; most city's educational trajectories are about constant turnover and discontinuous reforms.

Developmental intervention is, by definition, a sustained, multiyear effort. It requires regular, well matched infusions of expertise; changes to how central office works; shifts in thinking about the personnel needed to run a school well; and insulation from disruption. All of this work means that school boards, like unions, need some convincing. They either make the sorts of decisions needed for effective developmental intervention or must support their top administrators to pursue this work. If the board pursues its own agenda or doesn't understand that schools and districts haven't *ever* been organized to ensure excellent first instruction for every child, no form of intervention will work. In this case, closures and fire sales might really be the best option.

But this isn't going to happen. Charter schools are still a movement on the periphery, and most communities won't ever be led by a union-busting maverick superintendent with millions in private funding. Most low-performing schools are just like Stoddard, Tanner, and Connington. They're average. They need a way to work within the rules to produce the excellence their communities want.

So another tenet of developmental intervention holds that the imperative of joint learning can only come with an educated, supportive school board and that only one actor in the intervention business is in any position to provide this guidance: the state. School boards need to know about the stages of developmental of low-performing schools as much as principals do. They need information about which actions make the most sense, given a school's position on the way to internal accountability. They need to support and fund the construction of their district's instructional foundation. School boards should understand that the call for instructional leadership is not just rhetorical; it requires an organizational response, with new positions and new ways of supporting classroom-by-classroom improvement. For this work, the peg must be refashioned to fit the hole.

12. Guide Districts to Balance Short-Term and Long-Term Needs

In many ways, all the changes described here boil down to a real tension between the kind of responses incentivized by our current accountability and what we're learning about how schools achieve sustained growth in learning. On one hand, the uniform timelines encourage schools and districts to go for quick, sometimes marginal improvements. Tanner School made these kinds of moves: new test-taking strategies, test practicing camps on Saturdays, and remedial instruction for the lowest-performing students. On the other hand lie the more recent assertions that school turnaround is about long-term improvements to classroom teaching and about the ability of whole schools to learn and adapt in coherent ways. Of course, like so many arguments in public education, the dichotomy is false; low-performing schools are wise to pursue both routes. In fact, if the endeavor is fundamentally about organizational developmental—creating a culture of mutual expectations, inquiry, and support—then both approaches make sense. Both become matters of strategy, to be pursued in light the rough developmental pathway of similar schools.

Consequently, intervention has another important job to do—in an area that it currently treats silently. Intervention design must support more sophisticated conversations at every level about how short-term and long-term goals can complement one another and how they can sometimes work at cross purposes.

The creation of remedial programs—a very common response to state intervention—shows how this works.[5] At Tanner School, remediation was the central means by which the school hoped to escape its label as an underperforming school; at the Connington, students were grouped in elaborate ways throughout the school day, assigned to one of many levels for nearly every subject. Both schools had reasonable-sounding rationales for these practices. Less obvious, though no less important, however, was the eroding effect of these programs on teachers' sense of responsibility for improving the quality of the schools' core programs. The call for good first teaching, for grade-level content matched with differentiated methods, was reduced among teachers. At Tanner, teachers just said they wished the principal well with all of "her" programs. At Connington, teachers complained that they never got the chance to teach their own students; they never got the chance to develop a more sophisticated craft.

So, in the absence of an explicit strategy for balancing the short-term impulse to create remedial programs and the long-term need to deliver high-quality first teaching to all students, what usually happens? Do teachers and school leaders view the two as complementary? Do they fixate on student grouping and remedial curricula as long-term fixes? Left unprompted, do they consider the difference at all?

As a second example of the importance of seeing the short term in light of the long term, consider what happens when districts and schools choose to change out their instructional materials as a way of getting better. According to a recent report, 70 percent of intervention schools elect to do just this. In fact, in states like California, it's a requirement. We've already discussed one problem with the approach, given that most schools have no way of knowing how well their original program was enacted—or whether it was at all. But there's another potential problem to consider: Low-performing schools can often stall out or require time to consolidate their learning.[6] A developmental approach to intervention would at least pause on the question of whether a slate of new programs—and all the time, money, and support they require—further the cause of better first teaching. Is the content of the program so much better that it justifies the risk of diverting attention from the challenge of developing consistency with better methods? Does an improving school actually sometimes need time *without* change so that it can ensure consistency and quality with its current goals, before it takes its next step forward? In a one-size-fits-all system, there's little point to examining this issue; schools make changes to their programs all together, because it's cheaper to purchase the materials in bulk or because the school board needs symbolic change.[7] In an intervention system attuned to the developmental nature of school improvement, this level of discernment ought to be possible.

A Developmental Approach
to Intervention

H as nothing worked, then? Has the last generation of forays into low-performing schools produced nothing more than a few high-performing outliers, an even more impassioned interest in skirting the mire of traditional schools by moving to charters, a strengthening call for national standards and tests, and thousands of untouched low-performing schools? What about the effects of the instructional coaching, the attention to instructional leadership, the small-schools initiatives, and the millions of dollars in seed money? Hasn't any of this worked, or are we no further along in providing all children with a quality education?

Fortunately, we don't need to start from scratch with intervention or with the larger project of understanding and spreading effective instruction. Just as they have been all along, teaching and learning lie at the core of the work. We do need to acknowledge, though, that all the signals, labels, and sanctions—even when these things are turned up to boil—have had little effect on what happens in too many classrooms. For many teachers, the whole accountability regimen is patently antichild, and resistance to doing the wrong thing for kids has a rich history in American education. One can disagree with teachers' view of accountability and intervention, but this disagreement doesn't alter the fact that in this country, we own a school system—a big, locally controlled, high-friction system—in which the right to exercise a veto may as well be stapled to every classroom door. It's this reality, or school leader's fear of it, that explains some of what's going wrong.

This is only a small part of the issue, though. Resistance is a pretty cheap explanation for what's going on in low-performing schools. A better explanation is that accountability and intervention have so far not held that organizational development and professional learning are the central challenges to improving student learning. These systems have instead focused on shaping teachers' motivations, something more in line with classical economics than cognitive theory. So we can keep what we've got—but with far more support and far smarter thinking about how to help.

A new set of school intervention principles proposes the support of professional learning and problem solving by the people and agencies charged with this task—something far more akin to a client-consultant model than what we have right now. Distressingly, at all of the schools profiled in this book, central offices and state departments of education were most often portrayed by principals and teachers as another factor complicating their work. These were the sources of seemingly endless requests for information, of constrained choices, and of the enforcement of rules that appeared arbitrary. In its extreme, at Tanner School, the district's obligations to the state washed over the school's own particular needs and pretty well obviated the chance that teachers would embrace any homegrown efforts to improve. At Connington, Principal Jesse Martinez and his staff were alone to discover or invent the next round of improvement activities, without any guidance from district personnel. In these cases, district services mostly took the form of transactions related to financial and personnel matters; the professional-learning needs of the school were largely delegated to the sites, decentralized nearly to the point of desertion.

So what would it have looked like if the Stoddard, Tanner, and Connington schools had encountered a different kind of intervention, a developmental intervention? How would their stories have changed? How would their outcomes have been better? Let's consider a few issues that were most challenging for these schools.

How Developmental Intervention Could Help

Each of the three schools in this book started its interaction with the state in roughly the same condition, although one of these schools made steps forward while other two did not. Though the details were different, all the schools faced roughly the same dilemmas and challenges—with roughly the same undifferentiated expectations from the state Department of Education. In these earliest stages, all of the schools struggled with how to make sense of their underperformance—and usually looked to deficits in their students, families, and underserved communities. The principals in these schools all strove to shift this kind of thinking, and they did so with a good deal of variation. Principal Waighn skirted the question and launched remedial programs after school; Principal Martinez drove more forcefully toward changes in the classroom. Stoddard's Ken Schumer drew from instructional techniques that represented the lowest common denominator for his staff, while Martinez pursued large grants and new instructional materials. From the same set of dilemmas, each school invented its own way forward, all sharing the single fact that they were in this work by themselves, with no road maps, no guidance, and no awareness of what could reasonably be expected to come.

A developmental approach to intervention could have altered some of these early outcomes—or at least increased the efficiency with which these schools addressed the predictable anger, deflection, and pain of the early stages of intervention. Suppose that the principals of these schools had been afforded the advantage of training—with the follow-up support and coaching that we know to be a necessary part of adult learning—about the approximate stages of development in low-performing schools, their hallmark features, their pitfalls, and their opportunities. Suppose that the teachers in these schools, along with their union leaders, central office support providers, and school board members, also had enjoyed a similar advantage—not so much to peek into the future as to be grounded in how this process generally seems to proceed.

The people at Connington School got farthest along this road, but they mapped the route themselves, and one can gauge in hindsight whether the combative approach paid off. The school did choose the highly structured Reading First grant, but greatly lessened any prospect for ongoing professional learning, because of the years of turnover and acrimony. Even its best teachers, years later, didn't know if they could open their mouths during a meeting. If establishing the instructional foundation is a prelude to teachers' informed discretion, then Martinez and the other principals shouldn't have had to build it on their own. If teachers' informed discretion is where the school needed to head, then they should have had help building the routines and opportunities for meaningful collaboration. Expertise at the right time, on the right topic, would have made a big difference. As it was, these things were left unearthed.

Now imagine that Jesse Martinez, operating with a developmental base of knowledge and in concert with a developmental intervention team, hadn't committed to cleaning house at Connington. Suppose he hadn't forced the question of attribution back on his veteran staff with such vehemence, so that even seven years later, with mostly new teachers on board, too many of the school's meetings ran in silence and fear. Keeping in mind that trust and professional discretion would ultimately be the key resources of his school, Martinez and his developmental support team could have instead thoughtfully constructed the instructional foundation for the school: pacing guides for teachers so that meetings of teachers made sense; formative assessments so that teachers had a better window on their students' learning; a description of powerful teaching that drew from the best of old and new practice; a well-reasoned course of training and support on a smart synthesis of teaching for different groups of students. Imagine if the district's human resource department, after a year of this work, began to work with Martinez to find alternatives for the teachers who were clearly not going along, and if central office began to protect the school from the transportation rules, advanced placement programs, and disproportionate concentrations of ELL and special education students that systematically disadvantaged Connington. The school might not have imploded; it might not have been necessary, from the perspective of a serious principal, to force its implosion.

At Stoddard, a similar incremental approach would also have a made a real difference. In this school, the hallmark of its earliest work—besides the predictable infighting about what was causing their problems—was the search for strategies that drew exclusively from teachers' own thinking. Stoddard shouldn't have been in this situation. The default position of state intervention should have been that certain strategies would work better than others for schools like Stoddard and that these strategies could be named, taught, and supported until they were in widespread use. The problem at Stoddard was that everything had to change all at once, with the result that nothing changed at all. The state expected proficient data analysis, functional teams, strategic thinking, and instructional monitoring in its first year of work with the school. It got far less than this for all its imploration.

All this discussion assumes a real knowledge in education about what good teaching looks like, and that someone—the intervening body—should possess this knowledge. This means getting over the decade-long hang-up that such matters are best settled at the local level. The answers to low student performance cannot be coaxed from the schools themselves. In fact, it was unfair to make this assumption from the start. Intervention, as much as it must build problem-solving skills in anticipation of the really excellent, adaptive teaching these schools need, must infuse early-stage schools with real expertise about teaching. Fortunately, this isn't new work; there are groups that do this kind of work and do it very well: Research for Better Teaching (in Massachusetts), WestEd's Teach for Success, and the National Board for Professional Teaching Standards come to mind. These groups have all developed sound descriptions of good teaching, with a solid draw-from-the-best methodology, and they have their immediate application in struggling schools.

To infuse a school with this kind of knowledge for the purpose of establishing a baseline of proficient instruction is a long way from an expensive new set of textbooks and represents just the kind of investment in quality teaching that should come at the front end of a multiyear process like intervention. If somewhere down the line low-performing schools must achieve a baseline of instructional practice—a line below which no classroom teacher can drop—then the groundwork for establishing this baseline should start early. By a baseline of instructional practice, I mean a developmental stage—a common set of effective instructional strategies that schools should strive for. This means eliminating the ethic of unrestrained autonomy that defines so many schools. And this early work shouldn't happen at the expense of the school's reserve of trust; this is about expanding the practice of the professionals who have worked for a great many years in deep isolation. A developmental approach to intervention would have positioned the Stoddard, Tanner, and Connington schools very differently in this regard.

In the early stages of intervention, the schools in this book were most troubled by fights about why they were targeted by the state and felt alone in their efforts to undo their accountability status. Later, though, Connington and Stoddard came to a different set of problems—how to monitor instruction and how to achieve the sort of trust and knowledge that would allow for ongoing, strategic adaptation. As we've learned about these slightly more advanced stages, the dilemmas are still omnipresent, though their daily resolution, one hoped, would more and more favor the acceptance of responsibility, shared leadership, and efforts to improve every classroom in the school. Connington and Stoddard had a long way to go in these efforts.

Recall that even after years, these schools lurched around a great deal as they came up with new things to try. In the parlance of state intervention, they were all engaged in strategy selection or instructional monitoring, but the terms imply that the schools were matching known problems with known solutions. In reality, there was little of the sort going on. After seven years of state intervention, Reading First, and a three-tiered reading program, Connington finally arrived at a stage labeled by teachers, with no small measure of derision, as "serendipity." They were counting on the fourth-grade's team meetings and personal reading as the source of the next big idea. Stoddard submitted its improvement plan to the state having chosen from the most palatable practices already in the school. Tanner's teachers left the job to the principal, who in turn left the job to the superintendent.

Here again, the hoped-for outcomes might have happened if the basic principles of state intervention at the time had skewed toward developmental awareness and support. At Stoddard, for example, the teachers on the leadership team would have been loath to regularly inspect their colleagues' teaching. This cardinal prohibition among teachers turned out to be a blasting cap at the school. A developmental approach to intervention, one that was serious about collaboration and problem solving, would have approached this problem differently. Imagine a team composed of district, state, school, and even union leaders, involved in regular school visits and organizational coaching. Picture the basis of these frequent visits as a common definition for good teaching, with a multiyear base of training and support for all teachers. Imagine a newly created position for a new hire whose sole purpose was instructional improvement and who could stay removed from all the interruptions of a busy school. Envision a more tightly coordinated set of obligations to the central office, with less redundancy and less busy work. And most important, suppose that Stoddard had enjoyed the advantage of a developmental strategy, with guidance and expertise about what practices to employ toward the resolution of specific developmental problems. The school would still have had painstaking work ahead of it, but in a system more sensitive to developmental needs, this work would have been more focused, deliberate, and efficient. If there was movement in the wrong direction, it might not have lasted as long. If a stall occurred, it might not have been so disheartening.

In the context of an intervention aimed at working toward a high-functioning end state, with a developmental plan, team support, and some well-timed expertise, these misfires are less likely to occur. Developmentally, none of these schools were well positioned to begin collecting information about classroom teaching. If the challenge of monitoring had been previewed for these schools, however, and if these staffs had enjoyed the chance to learn how to do this work, then a year or two out, these schools could have pulled it off. They could have worked through the politics and the mistrust and could have put a base of good training beneath them. They could have worked with some instructional foundation from the district—a set of pacing guides, assessments, key standards, and maybe even well-written objectives or lessons. They could have invested some time in developing intervention and after-school programs that hit a bit farther from home for teachers. And most important, they could have done all these things *consciously*, with the support of their developmental intervention team. If the schools burned precious years trying to get to this point, anyway (and never making it), what did they have to lose in approaching intervention stepwise? As the adage says, sometimes you need to go slow to go fast.

For school communities that are past the self-reckoning of the earliest stages of intervention, we're learning that some efforts are better than others in helping to push classroom-by-classroom excellence. Schools should know exactly what these efforts are and should pursue them as a matter of strategy, not as a matter of luck.

Connecting All the Random Parts with a Developmental Strategy

The next generation of intervention in schools—a developmental intervention—needs to do better than what we've seen over the last ten years. States must do more to organize schools and districts into problem-solving teams, separating them from the silos that are so traditional in most central offices, so that isolation is no longer the norm. These teams need good, meaningful information about the developmental features of each school they serve and a strategy that is staged, well matched, and knowledge-rich.

The intervention experiences of low-performing schools so far suggest that there is something missing—some critical, still untested variable—in the current form of external accountability and intervention.

Fundamentally, schools cannot get better at what they do in such isolation and without some form of guidance as they necessarily grapple with the key dilemmas associated with their position as underperforming schools. There may be no way around these dilemmas, which seem to be the unavoidable consequence of introducing high-stakes tests, pressure, and timelines to large numbers of schools with limited capacity for sustained improvement. We must, however, be able to learn from these schools, and thoughtful changes to the current formulation of intervention would make these dilemmas less vexing for teachers and principals. We must find the next generation of intervention in low-performing schools so that we increase the probability of the outcomes the accountability movement was intended to produce. Inasmuch as these schools lack an encompassing sense of where they are going and how they can get there, this missing resource must provide both a general guide for improvement, and a better set of operating principles for coherently confronting each day's trade-offs.

As with any theory of development, low-performing schools' access to expertise must be continual and evolving. At each stage of their development, low-performing schools need coaching that is sensitive to their changing profile, to their evolving dilemmas, and to the provisional quality of their work. If there is no definitive map for improving underperforming schools, then one must hope for the services of a knowledgeable guide.

For better or worse, future intervention must evolve from its current position—with large numbers of schools approaching the terminal stages of their state's accountability systems and still relatively few success stories. The experiences of the Stoddard, Tanner, and Connington schools tell us that pressure alone is not likely to produce the changes that policy makers hope for. Schools such as these will not come up with the formula for success on their own; guesswork, even with the annual data from standardized testing, is still guesswork. Very sadly, the experiences of these three schools tell us that even a decade of being labeled underperforming may not be enough to improve a school.

Although most intervention today is missing a significant developmental strategy, the current crop of improvement activities—things like data analysis, coaching for teachers, and extra programming for struggling students—is not ineffective. Far from it. Each of these strategies still appears to hold great promise, and with time, they might eventually pay off at low-performing schools. Unfortunately, however, there is no clear signal from any source about how to use all these strategies in concert and how to ensure that they support the developmental goals of each school at a particular point in time. The boats may all be in the water, but they're not charting the same course. In the whirlwind of activity that is every school day, reading this course is proving to be improbably difficult.

In the end, the challenge of school intervention is fundamentally about instructional expertise and organizational development—about creating the culture of mutual expectations, support, and professional learning that leads to sustained growth in student understanding. Without radical and very unlikely changes to the architecture of public schools, there is simply no way around the dilemmas built into these schools. Schools will always face powerful problems related to the competition between stability and change. And these problems will always have to be resolved, over and over, by the people who work in each school. A decade of watching has shown that this is very hard work. It's so hard that the odds of dramatic improvement in many schools are unacceptably low. It may always be a game of odds, but we can't be content with this spread.

The problem is that education policy can't get into the fabric of schools to help resolve these dilemmas any more consistently or efficiently. Intervention policy won't ever succeed in "teacher-proofing" the work of educating students, or "principal-proofing" the work of leading teachers. But the next generation of intervention policy can take a developmental view of how low-performing schools appear to improve. It can help districts align their responsibilities and services to the needs of groups of developmentally similar schools, much as an excellent teacher does with his or her students. Improved intervention can learn from the details of schools like Stoddard, Tanner, and Connington, and by starting with an accurate understanding of the challenges inside actual low-performing schools, intervention policy can be more discerning and more helpful. The teachers and principals in these schools are well worth the effort, as is a renewed effort to influence the learning outcomes of so many thousands of our children.

Notes

Introduction

1. K. Laguarda, "State-Sponsored Technical Assistance to Low-Performing Schools: Strategies from 9 States," paper presented at annual meeting of the American Education Research Association, Chicago, April 21–25, 2003.
2. Leslie F. Hergert, Sonia Caus Gleason, Carole Urbano, and Charlotte North, *How Eight State Education Agencies in the Northeast and Islands Region Identify and Support Low-Performing Schools and Districts* (Issues & Answers Report, REL 2009, no. 068), U.S. Department of Education, Institute of Education Sciences, National Center for Education Evaluation and Regional Assistance, Regional Educational Laboratory Northeast and Islands, Washington, DC, March 2009.
3. Larry Abramson, "KIPP, Union Disagree on Baltimore Teachers' Pay," *Morning Edition,* National Public Radio, September 8, 2009.
4. Center on Education Policy, "Moving Beyond Identification: Assisting Schools in Improvement," report, Center on Education Policy, Washington, DC, July 2007, summarized the efforts of hundreds of districts to assist their low-performing schools. The list of improvement activities cited in this report corresponds closely with the efforts of the three schools in this book and includes such common endeavors as data analysis, coaching for teachers, the replacement of instructional programs, remedial and intensive programs, and professional development.
5. R. Elmore, "Bridging the Gap Between Standards and Achievement: The Imperative for Professional Development in Education," report, Albert Shanker Institute, Washington, DC, 2002; and R. Elmore, "Knowing the Right Thing to Do: School Improvement and Performance-Based Accountability," National Governors Association, Center for Best Practices, Washington, DC, August 2003.

Chapter 1

1. All personal names related to the case study schools in this book are pseudonyms.
2. J. O'Day, "Complexity, Accountability, and School Improvement," Harvard Education Review 72, no. 3 (fall 2002): 293–329
3. At the time of my interviews at the Stoddard School, 220 was the minimum score that students in Massachusetts had to achieve to be considered proficient. This score has since been raised to 240 on a scale from 200 to 280.
4. As part of PIM, the Stoddard team adopted from the school's external coach a visual model for developing a five-sentence paragraph. The model was shaped like a hamburger, with the lead and concluding sentences acting as the bread in a sandwich, and supporting content as the sandwich's inner layers.

Chapter 3

1. In 2006, the Massachusetts Department of Education suspended its use of Performance Improvement Mapping and entered a two-year study period on the problem of low-performing schools. During this study period, there was no school inspection process and no mechanism for providing feedback or guidance to low-performing schools.
2. S. Kardos et al., "Counting on Colleagues: Teachers' Experience of Professional Culture," paper presented at American Educational Research Association annual meeting, New Orleans, April 2000.

Chapter 4

1. J. McRobbie, "Can State Intervention Spur Academic Turnaround?" WestEd Policy Program, San Francisco, 1998, 2.
2. S. Mead, "Easy Way Out: Restructuring Usually Means Little Has Changed," *Education Next* (winter 2007); Center on Education Policy, "Moving Beyond Identification: Assisting Schools in Improvement," Center on Education Policy, Washington, DC, July 2007; and C. Mazzeo and I. Berman, "Reaching New Heights: Turning Around Low-Performing Schools," Education Policy Studies Division, National Governors Association, Washington, DC, 2003.
3. R. Elmore, "Knowing the Right Thing to Do: School Improvement and Performance-Based Accountability," National Governors Association, Center for Best Practices, Washington, DC, August 2003.
4. D. Holdzkom, "Low-Performing Schools: So You've Identified Them—Now What?" policy brief, AEL, Charleston, WV, 2001; and J. Feldman and R. Tung, "Whole School Reform: How Schools Use Data-Based Inquiry and Decision Making Process," Center for Collaborative Education, Boston, 2001.
5. Elmore, "Knowing the Right Thing to Do"; and H. Mintrop and A. MacLellan, "School Improvement Plans in Elementary and Middle Schools on Probation," *Elementary School Journal* 102, no. 4 (2002).
6. H. Mintrop, "The Limits of Sanctions in Low-Performing Schools: A Study of Maryland and Kentucky Schools on Probation," *Education Policy Analysis Archives* 11, no. 3 (2003); C. Abelmann and S. Kenyon, "Distractions from Teaching and Learning: Lessons from Kentucky's Use of Rewards," paper, Annual Meeting of the American Educational Research Association, New York, 1996; and K. Wong and F. Shen, "City and State Takeover As a School Reform Strategy," *ERIC Digest* 174 (July 2002).
7. Mazzeo and Berman, "Reaching New Heights"; Mintrop, "The Limits of Sanctions in Low-Performing Schools"; and D. Massell, "State Strategies for Building Capacity in Education: Progress and Continuing Challenges," *Research Report Series RR-41,* Consortium for Policy Research in Education, Philadelphia, 1998.
8. Mintrop and MacLellan, "School Improvement Plans"; and J. O'Day, "Complexity, Accountability, and School Improvement," *Harvard Educational Review* 72, no. 3 (fall 2002): 293–329.
9. Elmore, "Knowing the Right Thing to Do."
10. For an explanation of internal capacity, see M. Carnoy, R. Elmore, and L. Siskin, *The New Accountability: High Schools and High-Stakes Testing* (New York: Routledge-Falmer, 2003).
11. Ibid.

12. J. Gray, "Causing Concern but Improving: A Review of Schools' Experiences," London Department of Education and Employment Research Series, 2002.

13. Elmore, "Knowing the Right Thing to Do"; and D. Figlio and C. Rouse, "Do Accountability and Voucher Threats Improve Low-Performing Schools?" *Journal of Public Economics* 90, no. 1-2 (January 2006): 239–255.

14. Elmore, "Knowing the Right Thing to Do"; and Carnoy, Elmore, and Siskin, *The New Accountability.*

15. C. Galluci, "Communities of Practice and the Mediation of Teachers' Responses to Standards-Based Reform," *Education Policy Analysis Archives* 11, no. 35 (2003); and L. Siskin, "When an Irresistible Force Meets an Immovable Object: Core Lessons About High Schools and Accountability," in Carnoy, Elmore, and Siskin, *The New Accountability.*

16. R. Elmore, "Professional Networks and School Improvement: The Medical Rounds Model, Applied to K–12 Education, Provides a Community of Practice Among Superintendents Committed to Better Instruction," *School Administrator,* April 2007; and K. Wong and A. Nicotera, Successful Schools and Educational Accountability Concepts and Skills to Meet Leadership Challenges, *Peabody College Education Leadership Series* (Boston: Allyn & Bacon, 2006).

17. Elmore, "Knowing the Right Thing to Do."

18. Wong and Nicotera, *Successful Schools and Educational Accountability Concepts*; and J. Mauriel, "Instructional Leadership: Providing Quality Educational Services," in *Strategic Leadership for Schools: Creating and Sustaining Change,* Education Resource Information Center (ERIC) database no. ED319127 (San Francisco: Jossey-Bass, 1989).

19. R. Elmore, "On Good Schools, Failing Schools, and School Improvement: Interview by John Graham," *Professional Voice* 4, no. 2 (2006).

20. Wong and Nicotera, *Successful Schools and Educational Accountability Concepts.*

21. P. Rettig, *Practicing Principals: Case Studies, In-Baskets, and Policy Analysis* (Lanham, MD: Rowman & Littlefield Education, 2004); and J. Archer, "Tackling an Impossible Job," *Education Week,* September 15; and P. Sebring and A. Bryk, "School Leadership and the Bottom Line in Chicago," *Kappan,* February 2000, 440–443; and F. Hess, *Tough Love for Schools: Essays on Competition, Accountability, and Excellence* (Washington, DC: American Enterprise Institute, 2006); and A. Piccuci, "Driven to Succeed: High-Performing, High-Poverty, Turnaround Middle Schools," research report, University of Texas, Austin, 2002.

22. R. Sagor, "Developing a District and School Accountability System: Rationale and Sample Materials," Region III Comprehensive Center, George Washington University, Washington, DC, 2001.

23. M. LaRocque, "Closing the Achievement Gap: The Experience of a Middle School," *The Clearing House* (Heldof Publications) 80, no. 4 (2007).

24. S. M. Johnson, *Leading to Change: The Challenge of the New Superintendency* (San Francisco: Jossey-Bass, 1996).

25. P. Bredeson and B. Kose, "Responding to the Education Reform Agenda: A Study of School Superintendents' Instructional Leadership," *Education Policy Analysis Archives,* 15, no. 5 (2007):1–24; and C. Tolbert "Principals As Change Agents," unpublished dissertation, Harvard University, Cambridge, MA, 2002; and J. Spillane et al., "Managing in the Middle: School Leaders and the Enactment of Accountability Policy," *Educational Policy* 16, no. 5 (2002).

26. Elmore, "Knowing the Right Thing to Do."

27. K. Mitchell, "Reforming and Conforming: NASDC Principals Discuss School Accountability Systems" New American Schools Development Corporation, 1997; and H. Ladd, and A. Zelli, "School-Based Accountability in North Carolina: The Responses of School Principals," *Educational Administration Quarterly* (2002); and J. Lyons and B. Algozzine, "Perceptions of the Impact of Accountability on the Role of School Principals," *Education Policy Analysis Archives* 14, no. 6 (2006).

28. Elmore, "Knowing the Right Thing to Do."

29. Education Commission of the States, "Quality Counts: A Better Balance," *Education Week* special edition, 2001; and O'Day, "Complexity, Accountability, and School Improvement"; and D. Linn, B. Rothman, and K. White, "State Strategies for Turning Around Low-Performing Schools," National Governors Association Center for Best Practices, Washington, DC, 2003.

30. C. Scott "What Now? Lessons from Michigan About Restructuring Schools and Next Steps Under NCLB," Center on Education Policy, Washington, DC, 2007.

31. O'Day, "Complexity, Accountability, and School Improvement"; and P. Reville, "Examining State Intervention Capacity: How Can States Better Support Low-Performing Schools and Districts?" policy brief, Rennie Center for Education Research and Policy, Cambridge, MA, summer 2004.

32. C. Ascher, K. Ikeda, and N. Fruchter, "Schools on Notice: A Policy Study of New York State's 1996–1997 SURR Process," Institute for Education and Social Policy, New York University, 1998; Scott, "What Now?"; O'Day, "Complexity, Accountability, and School Improvement"; D. Phenix, "A Forced March for Failing Schools: Lessons from the New York City Chancellor's District," *Education Policy Analysis Archive* 13, no. 40 (2005); J. Snipes, F. Doolittle, and C. Herlihy, *Foundations for Success: Case Studies of How Urban School Systems Improve Student Achievement* (Washington, DC: Council of the Great City Schools, 2002); and E. Travers, "Philadelphia School Reform: Historical Roots and Reflections on the 2002–2003 School Year Under State Takeover," *Penn GSE Perspectives in Urban Education* 2, no. 2 (2003).

33. S. Yeh, "Limiting the Unintended Consequences of High Stakes Testing," *Education Policy Analysis Archives* 13, no. 43 (2005); and S. Caitlin, "Wrestling with the Devil in the Details: An Early Look at Restructuring in California," Center on Education Policy, Washington, DC, 2006.

34. Snipes, Doolittle, and Herlihy, *Foundations for Success*; Phenix, "A Forced March for Failing Schools"; Yeh, "High Stakes Testing"; O'Day, "Complexity, Accountability, and School Improvement"; K. Bitter, *Evaluation Study of the Immediate Intervention/ Underperforming Schools Program of the Public Schools Accountability Act of 1999* (Washington, DC: American Institute for Research, 2005); C. Reeves, "State Support to Low Performing Schools," Council of Chief State School Officers, Washington, DC, 2003; and D. Phenix, D. Siegel, A. Zaltsman, and N. Fruchter, "Virtual District, Real Improvement: A Retrospective Evaluation of the Chancellor's District, 1996–2003," NYU Institute for Education and Social Policy, New York, 2004.

Chapter 5

1. Center on Education Policy, "Moving Beyond Identification: Assisting Schools in Improvement," Center on Education Policy, Washington, DC, July 2007.

2. A. Bryk and B. Schneider, *Trust in Schools: A Core Resource for Improvement* (New York: Russell Sage Foundation, 2002).

3. G. Meeks and T. Stepka, "State-Wide Middle Level Implementation: Lessons Learned," *Research in Middle Level Education Online* 29, no. 3 (2004).

Chapter 6

1. J. O'Day, "Complexity, Accountability, and School Improvement," *Harvard Educational Review* 72, no. 3 (fall 2002): 293–329; and M. S. Mills, Ensuring the Viability of Curriculum Mapping in a School Improvement Plan," 2001, ERIC database, ED460141.

2. D. Conley, "Strategic Planning in Practice: An Analysis of Purposes, Goals, and Procedure," paper presented at Annual Meeting of the American Education Research Association, Atlanta, April 1993, ERIC database ED358530; and W. McInery and J. Leach, "School Improvement Planning: Evidence of Impact," *Planning and Change* 23, no. 1 (1992): 15–28.

3. J. Bransfors, A. Brown, and R. Cocking, eds., *How People Learn: Brain, Mind, Experience, and School* (Washington, DC: National Research Council, National Academy Press, 1999).

4. J. Armstrong and K. Anthes, "Identifying the Factors, Conditions, and Policies That Support Schools' Use of Data for Decisionmaking and School Improvement," Education Commission of the States, Denver, 2001.

5. Ibid.

6. R. Elmore, "Bridging the Gap Between Standards and Achievement: The Imperative for Professional Development in Education," Albert Shanker Institute, Washington, DC, 2002, available at www.shankerinstitute.org/education.html.

7. For an excellent analysis of the effect of school-board-related politics on public school systems, see F. Hess, *Spinning Wheels: The Politics of Urban School Reform* (Washington, DC: Brookings Institution Press, 1999).

About the Author

D. Brent Stephens is currently the principal of Anthony Ochoa Middle School in Hayward, California. He has also served as a K–8 principal in Somerville, Massachusetts; as a central office administrator in Lowell, Massachusetts; and as a Spanish bilingual teacher in Boston and Oakland, California. He holds a doctorate from the Urban Superintendents Program at the Harvard Graduate School of Education, and has earned certification by the National Board for Professional Teaching Standards.

Index

Note: Figures are indicated by "f" following the page number.

academic drop-in centers, 71–72
accountability
    internal, 123–125, 156, 166–169
    in low-performing schools,
        123–125
    NCLB and, 1
    teacher reactions to, 14–15, 25–26,
        53–58, 85–90, 109, 159–160,
        197
Adequate Yearly Progress (AYP),
    51–53
advanced-work programs, 112–113
after-school tutoring, 68–70
American Enterprise Institute, 159
assessment moments, 178
attribution
    administration's view of, 109
    as developmental dilemma, 14–15
    in developmental stages, 159–160
    to externalities, 109–114
    school orientation toward,
        150–152
    teacher response to, 24–26, 57,
        86–87, 150
authority. See control

baseline, of instruction, 163–164,
    201–202

Boston Public Schools, 192
Bryk, Anthony, 163

California, 10
Calkins, Lucy, 107
Carnoy, Martin, 121
centralized control, 15–16, 85, 90–91,
    94–99, 136, 152–153
central office silos, 178–181
change
    resistance to, 8, 47–48, 89
    stability versus, 137, 162, 174–175
charter schools, 5–6, 187
classroom intervention, 16–17, 153–
    155, 180–181
classroom learning objectives, 177–178
communication failures, 47–48
compliance
    dangers of, 12, 17, 30, 43, 121,
        132–133, 138–139, 141
    as developmental dilemma, 17,
        42–43, 119, 121, 122, 137–141,
        155–156
    with school district, 80–81
Composite Performance Index (CPI),
    67
control of instruction, 15–16, 85, 90–
    91, 94–95, 98–99, 136, 152–153

conversion partnerships, 5–6
curriculum, narrowing of, 55–56

data analysis
    in developmental intervention,
        189–192
    gathering data for, 155, 191
    for plan implementation, 36–37
    problems with, 23
    and use of data, 67, 190
databanks of instructional practices,
    190–191
demographic features
    PIM's disallowance of, 24–26
    and student performance, 53–54,
        87–88, 110–111, 150
development, instructional
    improvement as process of, 8,
        13–18, 121–123
developmental dilemmas, 13–18
    attribution, 14–15, 150–152
    classroom intervention, 16–17, 37,
        153–155
    compliance, 17, 137–141, 155–156
    control of instruction, 15–16, 98–99,
        152–153
    crucial, 14–17
    instructional improvement versus
        stability, 137, 162, 174–175
    as key obstacle to improvement,
        13–14
    responses to, 157f
    school orientation toward, 148–158
developmental intervention, 171–195
    benefits of, 199–204
    classroom delivery of instructional
        initiatives, 180–181
    data gathering, analysis, and use,
        189–192
    improvement planning, 181–183
    instructional foundation, 176–178

long-range plans, 173
    organizational tasks, 186–187
    politics, 192–193
    principals' duties, 183–186
    problem solving, 175–176
    prospects for, 197–207
    school district problems, 178–181,
        188–189
    short-term needs, 193–195
    staged implementation, 172–174
developmental profiles, 148–169
    administrative responses, 160–162
    attribution, 150–152
    classroom intervention, 153–155
    control of instruction, 152–153
    defining the challenge, 155–156
    developmental stages, 158–169
    internal accountability, 166–169
    reactions and attribution questions,
        159–160
    school identity, 164–166
    school orientation toward key
        dilemmas, 148–158
    voluntarism, 162–164
developmental stages
    administrative responses, 160–162
    determination of, 146–148
    internal accountability and sustained
        growth, 166–169
    reactions and attribution questions,
        159–160
    universalism and school identity,
        164–166
    voluntarism, 162–164
developmental strategy, 144–145
DIBELS. *See* Dynamic Indicators of
    Basic Early Literacy Skills
differentiated instruction, 58–60,
    64–65
director of instruction, 185
distributed control, 15–16, 85, 152–
    153

DOE. *See* Massachusetts Department of Education
drop-in centers, 71–72
Duncan, Arne, 1, 4–5
Dynamic Indicators of Basic Early Literacy Skills (DIBELS), 100–101

Education Commission of the States, 190
Elmore, Richard, 120, 121, 146, 158
examination schools, 112–113
externalities, blaming, 24–26, 109–114, 150. *See also* demographic features

first instruction, 179

Gray, John, 121–123, 146, 158
Green Dot Charter Schools, 5

Immediate Intervention/ Underperforming School Program (II/USP), 10
implementation, staged, 172–174
improvement planning, 181–183
incentives, ineffectiveness of, 175
inclusion, 59–60
innovation, 106–109
instruction
    best practices in, 190–191
    control of, 15–16, 85, 90–91, 94–95, 98–99, 136, 152–153
    core, 75–77, 162
    foundation for, 176–178
    relabeling of traditional practices in, 34, 45–46, 64–65
    school capacities for, 153
    test-driven, 55–57, 67, 101
    uniform methods of, 100–101
instructional core, 75–77, 162
instructional improvement. *See also* performance improvement mapping (PIM)
    commonalities in classroom delivery and, 180–181
    common methods of, 9–10
    contexts for, 8–11, 65, 118, 128
    creating administrative role for, 185–186
    crisis in, 1–4
    as developmental process, 8, 13–18, 121–123
    dilemmas as key obstacle in, 13–18
    failure of, 3–4
    nonlinear, 120–123
    obstacles to, 7
    transmission of best practices for, 190–191
    various approaches to, 199
instructional materials, changes in, 178, 195
internal accountability, 123–125, 156, 166–169
internal capacity, 121, 175
interventions. *See also* developmental intervention; performance improvement mapping (PIM)
    common mistakes, 41–48, 73–81, 103–114
    compliance with, 12, 17, 43
    context-specific, 11, 118, 128, 173–174
    problems in, 2, 12–13, 198
    resistance to, 47–48, 89, 132
isolation, professional, 9, 11, 31, 46–47, 102, 130–134, 163–164, 168–170

KIPP (Knowledge Is Power Program) charter schools, 6

leadership teams. *See* school leadership teams
lesson study, 177
long-range plans, 173, 193–195
Los Angeles Unified School District, 5
low-hanging fruit, instructional improvement strategy targeting, 122, 160–162
low-performing schools. *See also* school culture
accountability in, 123–125
autonomy of, 66
compliance culture in, 12, 17, 43, 137–141
consequences facing, 3
crisis of, 1–3
developmental dilemmas faced by, 13–18, 148–158
developmental stages of, 158–169
fundamental characteristics of, 7, 11, 118, 128–137
individual contexts of, 8–11, 52–53, 65, 118, 128
instability in, 134–137
isolation of, 9, 11, 31, 46–47, 102, 130–134, 163–164, 168–170
lack of preparation for instructional improvement in, 9, 11–12, 31, 190–191, 199, 201
leadership issues in, 125–127
maladaptive responses of, 121
needs assessment for, 143–170
needs of, versus district's needs, 79–81, 140, 179–180, 193–195, 198
nonlinear improvement in, 120–123
prevalence of, 3
school district influence on, 127–128

state influence on, 127–128
variations in, 119–128

Massachusetts, instructional improvement programs in, 9–10
Massachusetts Comprehensive Assessment System (MCAS), 30, 36, 51, 56–57, 62, 64, 66–67, 71, 84, 97, 100, 112
Massachusetts Department of Education (DOE)
lack of intervention by, 102
PIM administration by, 29–31, 35
PIM team perceptions of, 28–30
requirements for underperforming schools, 66, 89, 99–100, 117
Mass Insight, 159
McRobbie, Joan, 119
Menino, Tom, 192
Mintrop, Heinrich, 120, 146, 158
monitoring, 36–41

National Board for Professional Teaching Standards, 201
national standards, 4–5
needs assessment for low-performing schools, 143–170
developmental profiles, preparation of, 148–169
developmental stage, determination of, 146–148
developmental strategy, formulation of, 144–145
New York, 9–10
90-90-90 schools, 107
No Child Left Behind Act (NCLB)
accountability imposed by, 1
Obama administration and, 4
requirements of, 67
shortcomings of, 145
nonlinear improvement, 120–123

Obama administration, 4–6
O'Day, Jennifer, 179
organizational change, barriers to, 7

Payzant, Tom, 192
performance improvement mapping
    (PIM)
    attributions in, 24–26
    critical approach lacking in, 43–44
    data about implementation, 36–41
    data analysis in, 23
    document resulting from, 35–36
    guidance received by, 31
    inclusiveness in, 32–34
    monitoring phase in, 36–41
    objective of, 21–22
    politicization of, 45–46
    self-organization for, 35–36
    staff responses to, 22–24
    strategy selection, 30–35
    support for, 34
    team development for, 26–28
PIM. *See* performance improvement
    mapping
planning
    data analysis for, 36–37
    improvement, 181–183
    long-range, 173, 193–195
politics, 45–46, 192–193
principals
    challenges facing, 126
    control by, 90–91, 94–99
    developmental intervention
        involving, 183–186
    initiatives of, 58–59, 69–71, 95–97
    role and skills of, 125–127,
        183–186
    teacher-principal relations, 55, 61–
        63, 85, 94–95, 97–98, 132, 136
proactive thought, 44
problem solving, 175–176
professional development
    on differentiated instruction, 58–59
    inadequate, 105–106
    incorporation of, into instructional
        improvement, 32
    for instructional foundation, 176–
        177
    internal accountability and, 123–
        125
    isolation's effect on, 130–132

Race to the Top program, 4
Reading First, 89, 96, 98–100, 106
Research for Better Teaching, 201
resistance to change, 8, 47–48, 89, 132
Rhee, Michelle, 5

sanctions, ineffectiveness of, 175
school boards, 192–193
school culture
    administrative actions influencing,
        161
    resistance to change in, 8
    school identity and, 164–166
school districts
    administrative problems in, 178–
        181, 188–189
    criticisms of, 109–113
    inadequate responses by, 73–75
    and instructional leadership,
        77–79
    needs of, 79–81, 140, 179–180,
        193–195, 198
    recognition of failure patterns,
        73–75
    role of, 127–128
school identity, 164–166. *See also*
    school culture
school leadership teams, 27, 97
schools. *See* low-performing schools
Schools Under Registration Review
    (SURR), 10

school takeovers, 5
scripted reading program, 100, 105
seniority, among teachers, 33
sheltered English instruction (SEI)
    programs, 87–88, 111
special education, 87–88, 111
stability, schools' tendency toward,
    137, 162, 174–175
standards, national, 4–5
strategy selection, 30–35
    DOE directives for, 30–31
    inclusiveness in, 32–34
    internal focus of, 31–33
    mixture of old and new in, 32–33
    politicization of, 45–46
    presentation of, 34, 45–46
student assignment, 110–112
student learning objectives (SLOs), 30
student performance
    causes of, 24–26, 29–30, 53–54, 109
    middle-level, 68–69
    strategies for improving, 30–35
support providers, role of, 176

takeovers. *See* school takeovers
takeover teams, 5
teachers
    attitudes about student performance,
        24–26, 29–30
    autonomy of, 60–63, 70, 154, 167
    blaming of, 25
    dissatisfaction with instructional
        policies, 55–57, 67
    internal accountability of, 123–125,
        156, 166–169
    as key to improvement, 17–18
    monitoring as dilemma for, 36–41
    perceptions of DOE, 28–30
    performance judged by student test
        scores, 7

principal-teacher relations, 55, 61–
    63, 85, 94–95, 97–98, 132, 136
    reactions of, to accountability status,
        14–15, 25–26, 53–58, 85–90,
        109, 159–160, 197
    response of, to classroom
        intervention, 16–17, 153–155
    seniority among, 33
    trust in, 167
    turnover of, 90–94, 103–105
Teach for Success, 201
tenure reform, 5
Texas, 10
textbooks. *See* instructional materials
trust, 163, 167
tutoring, after-school, 68–70
21st Century Learning Center, 69–70,
    76

underperforming schools. *See* low-
    performing schools
unions
    and collective bargaining
        agreements, 37
    in KIPP schools, 6
    and principal-teacher problems, 62,
        94–95
    school custodians', 70
universalism, in instructional
    approach, 164–166
U.S. Department of Education, 4, 187

voluntarism, 162–164

walk-throughs, 40–41
WestEd, 201
workshop model for reading/writing
    instruction, 100